MAMETZ

MAMETZ

Lloyd George's 'Welsh Army'
at the Battle of the Somme

by

COLIN HUGHES

Today I found in Mametz Wood
A certain cure for lust of blood
Robert Graves

GLIDDON BOOKS

This 1990 edition published by Gliddon Books
First published privately by Orion Press in 1982

© A. C. Hughes 1982 and 1990

ISBN 0 947893 20 2
A CIP catalogue record card for this book is
available from the British Library

Cover design Ashwell Print Services

Printed and bound in Great Britain by
Biddles Ltd, Guildford and King's Lynn

Contents

Maps

List of Illustrations with acknowledgements

Between pages 96 *and* 97

Preface to the first edition

This is the story of the capture of Mametz Wood by the 38th (Welsh) Division in 1916. My interest in the subject began in 1946, when I first heard on the radio a dramatisation of David Jones's prose poem *In Parenthesis*, which tells of the fortunes of John Ball, a private soldier in a new army battalion of Londoners and Welshmen in the early years of the First World War. The climax is an attack on an unnamed wood in which John Ball is wounded and many of his companions are killed. The work made a deep impression on me and interest was rekindled some twenty years later when Jones's book, originally published in 1937, appeared in paperback form. At that time, I was working in the War Office building in Whitehall with access to its extensive range of First World War literature, and I was able, without difficulty, to identify the unit in which 'John Ball' served and the wood in which he fought. In the process, I came across Wyn Griffith's *Up to Mametz*, a book dealing with the same military unit (in which Griffith also served) and the same events. *Up to Mametz* was then out of print, but happily is now available again. My curiosity aroused, I visited and photographed some of the landscape featured in both works. These photographs brought an immediate response when I sent them to David Jones and Wyn Griffith, and this encouraged me to undertake the research on which this book is based.

The story that unfolded was fascinating. Both David Jones ('John Ball') and Wyn Griffith served in the London Welsh battalion of the Royal Welsh Fusiliers, one of twelve battalions in the 38th (Welsh) Division, raised by Lloyd George in a grandiose attempt to create a Welsh Army whose feats, he fondly imagined, would equal those of Welshmen at the Battle of Crecy. Lloyd George became president of the London Welsh battalion, in which both his two sons served. Friends and political aides were put into high levels of command in the division. The attack on Mametz Wood some 20 months later was regarded as a triumph and a disaster, a success and a failure, depending on the viewpoint of the observer.

The events at Mametz made a lasting impression on other poets and writers who happened to be in the vicinity: Siegfried Sassoon fought for Quadrangle Trench and Wood Trench below Mametz Wood a few days before the Welsh attack; Robert Graves and Frank Richards were on the spot soon afterwards. Gerald Brenan, passing by, entered the wood as the corpses were stiffening to green marble.

But apart from literary associations, the capture of Mametz Wood turned out to be an ideal subject for military study. It so happened that the wood was nearly one mile wide, approximately the length of line occupied by one division, and the attack was an isolated event; a prelude to a full scale assault on the ridge beyond. For a few days, all eyes were focussed on the Welsh division while the rest of the British army more or less stood still. An operation on such a manageable scale, with well defined boundaries and with a recognisable beginning and end, was unusual on the Western Front. It provides a rare opportunity for detailed analysis; for laying bare the whole pattern of events, from simple conception to confused and bloody conclusion.

To help the reader unfamiliar with the war in France, I have described in some detail the structure of the army in 1914 and the build up to the Battle of the Somme. This is well trodden ground and I make no pretence at originality; but without a knowledge of these things a full understanding of the part played by the Welsh division at Mametz would not be possible.

I should say something of the spelling of 'Welsh' in the titles of the Royal Welsh Fusiliers and the Welsh Regiment. In adopting what may seem to some a perverse spelling, I have followed the practice of Army Lists of the time. It is true that in earlier times, and since 1920, the Regiments used, and always favoured the spelling 'Welch', but during the First World War, and for a time afterwards, this was frowned upon by the War Office. When the new army battalions were raised, the official spelling was with an 's' and these battalions were dissolved before the older form was readopted. Furthermore, the contemporary records from which I quote extensively, used the 's' spelling and it would have been wilful·to make a change notwithstanding the present day reader's familiarity with 'Welch'. I have before me, as I write, a report of an attack on the German trenches in 1916. It is signed 'T. Elias, Captain and Adjutant, 15th Battalion Royal Welsh Fusiliers' which shows that in the new army battalions at least, local usage and War Office wishes coincided.

For abbreviations of military rank, I have relied wherever possible on the 1914 issue of the army's *Field Service Pocket Book*.

Acknowledgements

I have already mentioned the stimulus which came from the work of two distinguished writers who fought at Mametz Wood: David Jones and Wyn Griffith. In the later years of their lives, I received from both writers warm hospitality, invaluable advice and much encouragement. Most of the writing and the research was carried out under the supervision of Professor Arthur Marwick of the Open University, to whom I am deeply grateful. I am also much indebted to my colleague Mr T G T Taylor for his unfailing support and for suggesting many improvements to the text.

The Chief Librarian of the Ministry of Defence Library Services, Mr J C Andrews, provided facilities for research, and members of the library staff gave willing help at all times. Assistance was also received from the Archivist, Churchill College, Cambridge; the Keeper of Manuscripts, the National Library of Scotland; the Head of the Department of Printed Books, Imperial War Museum; the Deputy Director of the former Beaverbrook Library; and the staffs of the Public Records Office and the British Library, Newspaper Library.

Thanks go to my brother, Mr L P Hughes, who travelled many miles on my behalf to talk to survivors of the battle; to Mr R L Joseph for translating passages from German regimental histories; to Mr F Lloyd for the original cover design; and to Mr G W H Potts, whose skill with the typewriter I have never seen surpassed.

My greatest debt is to my wife, Gillian, who took on extra domestic burdens without complaint and helped in many other ways.

Acknowledgement is due to Faber and Faber Ltd for permission to reprint extracts from *In Parenthesis* by David Jones and *Memoirs of an Infantry Officer* by Siegfried Sassoon; to Hugh Wyn Griffith for extracts from *Up to Mametz* by Llewelyn Wyn

Griffith; to Constable and Co Ltd for extracts from *Sir Douglas Haig's Command* by G A B Dewar and J H Boraston; and to the Controller of Her Majesty's Stationary Office for extracts from the *Official History of the Great War: Operations in France and Belgium* and from papers in the custody of the Public Records Office. Where I have quoted briefly from other works, the source is given in the notes to the appropriate chapter.

Finally, I would like to acknowledge my dept to those survivors of the fighting who responded so generously to my enquiries. To them, and to the others who fought at Mametz Wood, this work is respectfully dedicated.

Preface to the new edition

Mametz was first published in 1982. For several years afterwards, I remained in touch with some of the survivors of the battle for Mametz Wood who had contributed to the story of its capture. The appearance of the book prompted others, whom I had previously failed to track down, to give me their recollections of the fighting in the wood, and one, Emlyn Davies, sent a copy of a privately published, highly readable narrative, *Taffy went to War*. This is an excellent record of one man's experiences with the Welsh division and I was glad to see that it did not contradict anything in *Mametz*. Of all the potential critics of *Mametz*, the veterans were the ones I feared most; these were the ones who would tell me where I had gone wrong. To my great relief, it seemed to 'pass muster' with them all.

Most of these survivors have now passed away, among them Tom Price, whose graphic account of the attack on the 'Hammerhead' at Mametz Wood appears on page 107 of this work. In 1983, sixty-seven years after his first fateful visit, Tom went back to Mametz Wood. It was a moving experience and he shed a few tears as old memories came flooding back. He was disappointed, however, to find no memorial to the Welsh division at Mametz and he resolved to take up the matter on his return to Wales.

He found a ready response in the South Wales branch of the Western Front Association which, with great energy and enthusiasm, raised funds, commissioned designs, and supervised the construction of a superb memorial on a site at Mametz generously donated by the Thezy family, the owners of the wood. The memorial, a defiant red dragon on a stone plinth, stands on high ground overlooking the southern edge of Mametz Wood and the war cemetery at Flatiron Copse. On 11 July 1987, the 71st anniversary of the capture of Mametz Wood, hundreds of Welsh, English and French people gathered for its dedication. A few survivors of the battle were there, but, alas, Tom Price was not among them. He died shortly before its completion; but he died knowing that the achievements of the Welsh division would long be revered.

The publication of a new edition enables me to correct some errors, to refine and clarify the text in a number of places, and to improve the presentation. Photographs are included for the first time. I was tempted to carry the narrative forward to include the Welsh division's other deeds in the first world war: at the third battle of Ypres in 1917; and, by great coincidence, at Mametz Wood again in 1918. At this second encounter on the Somme the German armies were in retreat. The Welsh division was able to sweep through Mametz Wood and also through High Wood and into the open ground beyond, advancing, in a few days, across all the ground fought for so desperately by the full weight of the Fourth Army in 1916 and subsequently lost again to the Germans. Such are the fluctuating fortunes of war. But extending the story in this way would have changed the nature of the book. *Mametz* is a detailed, and I hope vivid, account of one isolated event in the war. It takes the reader into the battle and into the wood, and by dispelling the 'thick air' of muddles and confusions aims to reveal what kind of a 'show' it was. It seems best to leave it that way.

I should like to thank Julie Hawes for secretarial assistance in the preparation of the new edition.

1. Lloyd George's Welsh Army

Pick those knees up.
Throw those chests out.
Hold those heads up.
Stop that talking.
Keep those chins in.
Left left lef' - lef' righ' lef' - you Private Ball it's you
I'v got me glad-eye on.

'War trembling in the balance' wrote Lloyd George to his wife on 28 July 1914. 'No one can tell what will or will not happen. I still believe peace will be preserved. The great powers will hesitate before they plunge their countries into the hell of war.'[1] That very day, Austria declared war on Serbia using the assassination of Archduke Francis Ferdinand, a month earlier, as a pretext. By 2 August, Russia, Germany and France had issued orders for general mobilisation and the German army was marching into Luxembourg. 'Europe is in arms,' proclaimed the military correspondent of *The Times*, 'and the greatest war of modern time is upon us.'[2]

As Lloyd George's letter reveals, the swiftness of events took Asquith's Liberal administration by surprise. Preoccupied with Ireland and concerned at the possibility of civil unrest at home, the Cabinet was slow to recognise the danger signs in Europe. Even when it did, the first reaction was to keep out of a Continental war at any price. As the crisis deepened, the Foreign Secretary, Sir Edward Grey, did what he could to restrain Germany from reckless action but by 28 July he was beginning to despair and spoke of 'some devilry going on in Berlin'.[3] Two days later, he thought the time had come 'to converse upon how we should conduct ourselves in war, no longer how war can be avoided'.[4] The Cabinet however was deeply divided and incapable of reaching any decision. Some members were strongly pacifist and found the prospect of war far too horrible to contemplate. A few, including Churchill and Haldane, were ready to intervene on the side of France. Most however were against such intervention at first, though they wavered, hourly becoming more and more convinced of the inevitability of war. For Lloyd George, who was Chancellor of the Exchequer, the decision was particularly agonising. He was not a pacifist in the strict sense of the word but he was usually counted in the peace lobby. He was against intervention - partly on economic grounds - but he was realist enough to know that if the Germans attacked the French Channel coast and the British Government took no action, public opinion would have 'swept them out of power in a week'.[5] Like others, he waited for, and perhaps welcomed, German violation of Belgian neutrality which would have a powerful effect on the British people and give him the excuse he needed to support Sir Edward Grey. When, on 2 August, news reached the Government that German troops were massing on the Belgian frontier the Cabinet was almost totally united and next morning sanctioned the mobilisation of the armed forces.

That afternoon, Sir Edward Grey put the case for intervention to the House of Commons. He appealed to each member to 'search his conscience' on the matter of Britain's obligation to France and reach his own conclusion. He dusted down Britain's complicated treaty with Belgium, and spoke of a moral, if not a legal, obligation to go to that country's defence. He spoke also of Britain's own self-interest. 'If we were to say that all those things mattered nothing, were as nothing, and to say that we would stand aside, we should, I believe, sacrifice our respect and good name and reputation before the world, and should not escape the most serious and grave economic consequences.'[6] This was an appeal that few could resist, and Grey carried the House of Commons with him. The next day, 4 August 1914, Britain was at war with Germany.

Lord Kitchener

Throughout this period, the country was effectively without a Secretary of State for War. In March 1914 Asquith had combined the post with the office of Prime Minister to restore confidence in the army following the political mishandling of an incident at the Curragh in Ireland in which the loyalty of some officers on the issue of Irish home rule had been called into question. Obviously, a full time Secretary of State for War was again required. At first, Asquith favoured Haldane, the Lord Chancellor, who had completed a long and successful spell in that capacity only two years before and who still took an interest in the army. During his six years at the War Office, Haldane had shaped the regular army at home into an efficient expeditionary force of six infantry divisions and a cavalry division, and had created from the old, ill-equipped Volunteers and Yeomanry, a well-organised part-time army of 14 infantry divisions and 14 cavalry brigades - the Territorial Force - for home defence.[7] When the Cabinet took its decision on 3 August 1914 to mobilise, it was Haldane who went to the War Office to set the wheels in motion, and it seemed natural that he should stay. The possibility of his reappointment however brought loud protests from *The Times* which was deeply suspicious of Haldane's unconcealed admiration for Germany and the German people. 'It is necessary,' *The Times* declared, 'that the army should be in the firm hands of a man in whom the public have confidence; and we do not know where we can find any head for the War Office who would more completely secure this confidence than Lord Kitchener. It is true that he has not an intimate aquaintance with the army at home...[but] Lord Kitchener is a capable administrator, and a first rate organiser.' And with some shrewdness, considering subsequent events, *The Times* added: 'He can also improvise new measures and deal faithfully with red tape'.[8] Haldane himself recommended Kitchener for the post, although the latter showed some reluctance to accept it.

Nevertheless, on 6 August, to the great delight of *The Times*, Asquith revealed that Kitchener had agreed to become Secretary of State for War 'without in any way identifying himself with any set of political opinions'.[9] Later on, this appointment was to prove disastrous, for Kitchener, a serving soldier in a political post, ran the War Office like a despot, consulting no one on either military or political affairs. But, for the moment, this former conqueror of the Sudan, Commander-in-Chief in South Africa, reformer of the Indian Army and ruler of Egypt carried enormous prestige. He dominated his colleagues in the Cabinet and inspired in his countrymen a belief that he could take the decisions which would lead them to victory.[10] There was no word of dissent in Cabinet when, contrary to the generally held view that the war would be over in a few months, Kitchener announced that it would be fought on a massive scale and might last for many years.

The British army, Kitchener firmly believed, was quite inadequate for this task. He made little allowance for the difficulties which his predecessors, in time of peace, had faced in shaping an instrument for war and he regarded their achievements with contempt. The Expeditionary Force might be well organised and well equipped, but it was ridiculously small. 'I am put here to conduct a great war,' he said, 'and I have no army.'[11] His view of the Territorial Force was equally jaundiced. He completely ignored its potential for development and saw only that it was under strength, partly trained and poorly equipped. Furthermore - and this seemed to damn it in his eyes - it was a 'Town Clerk' army, not fully under War Office control. Kitchener determined, therefore, to raise his own new army, or armies, building firmly on the foundation of the regular army, and not on the Territorials.

The New Armies

Kitchener arrived at the War Office on 6 August. That evening, Asquith asked Parliament on his behalf 'for the army, power to increase the number of men of all ranks, in addition to the number already voted, by no fewer than 500,000'. The contrast with Haldane eight years earlier could not have been more marked. It had taken Haldane more than 18 months to persuade Parliament to sanction the reorganisation of the auxiliary forces; it took Kitchener less than one day to obtain similar authority for the creation of an entirely new army of unprecedented size, and the only argument put forward in justification was that it was being done 'at his request'. Such was the confidence he inspired.

Although he would have welcomed power to raise his new army by conscription, Kitchener accepted the widely-held political view that compulsory service would not be tolerated by the British people even in time of war. On 7 August he appealed for 100,000 volunteers to join the regular army for a period of three years, or 'the duration' of the war.[12] The response was immediate and recruits came pouring in. The normal recruiting machinery, which had been built to cope with 30,000 recruits a year, was swamped with as many in less than a week. 'All the air was ringing with rousing assurances,' C E Montague recalled later, 'France to be saved, Belgium righted, freedom and civilisation rewon, a sour, crooked old world to be rid of bullies and crooks and reclaimed for straightness, decency, good-nature, the ways of common men dealing with common men. What a chance!'[13] At the London recruiting office in Great Scotland Yard the crowd of applicants grew so large that mounted police had to be called in to control it. Additional recruiting offices were quickly opened to deal with the flood and by late August 100,000 men had joined the army. During the first week in September the recruitment rate rose to 30,000 a day and it soon became necessary to ask Parliament to sanction the addition of another half-million men.

Meanwhile, Kitchener's plans for the army took shape. Nothing needed to be done to the British Expeditionary Force except to reinforce it with some units of the regular army serving abroad and to move it as quickly as possible to France. During the second week of the war, four of the six infantry divisions and the cavalry division of the BEF crossed the English Channel and took up a position on the left of the French army. The two other divisions soon followed. Indian Army units took over more of the garrison duties in British overseas territories and this released enough British troops to provide two new regular infantry divisions for France - numbered the Seventh and Eighth.

The Territorial Force, however, presented something of a problem. Kitchener has been criticized for not using the territorials as a base from which to build his new army, but he knew that the force needed some attention before any thought could be given to its expansion. Haldane was proud of the way in which he had built up the organisation from first principles, discarding many of the uncertainties that surrounded the old auxiliary forces. But one flaw remained. The primary role of the Territorial Force was home defence and there was no obligation on its members to serve abroad. It is true that Haldane had also seen it as a means of expanding the Expeditionary Force in time of need - and had guessed, rightly as it turned out, that there would be no shortage of volunteers for overseas service - but he failed to take account of the divisive effect this would have on individual units, each of which was certain to contain men unwilling, or unable, to leave the country.

Kitchener's first step, therefore, was to ask the administrating County Associations to reorganise the force into home service units 'to receive all those who cannot volunteer for foreign service' and foreign service units to which those 'who have not such important ties at home' would be transferred.

He instructed that priority in training should be given to the latter to bring them quickly to a 'standard of efficiency which would enable them to do credit to the British army on foreign service'.[14] Under these arrangements, the move of territorial divisions overseas began within a few weeks of the outbreak of war, the first three being used to relieve regular troops in the Mediterranean, Egypt and India, thus enabling three new regular divisions to be formed: the 27th, 28th and 29th. A few selected battalions were also sent to France a few months later to be brigaded with regular battalions, although full divisions were not sent until the Spring of 1915. Even so, this was months before the first of Kitchener's new army divisions was ready to take the same road.

Once these decisions had been taken, the Territorial Force itself was ready for expansion. On 21 September 1914, County Associations were authorised to form one 'second line' territorial unit for every unit going overseas. As new recruits automatically accepted liability for foreign service the earlier inflexibility of the Territorial Force in this respect gradually disappeared. By the end of the war, twenty two out of a total of twenty eight territorial divisions had served overseas.[15] This expansion took place, of course, in competition with the formation of the new army and given the attention and publicity lavished on the latter, it is not surprising that the Territorial Force came off second best. For every recruit joining the territorials, at least two went to the new army.[16]

Within days of launching his appeal for 100,000 volunteers, Kitchener had decided on the framework for his new force. Army Orders issued on 16 and 21 August authorised the addition to the army of six infantry divisions, the new battalions of which were to be raised within the existing regimental structure. Within the regiment, the new battalions would be numbered in sequence behind the existing regular and territorial battalions and would be distinguished from them by the inclusion of the word 'Service' after the number. The following example was given:

8th (Service) Bn the Royal Welsh Fusiliers.[17]

Thus was born the first new army.[18] Equal in size to the pre-war Expeditionary Force, it was made up of 80 new battalions drawn from their regiments and organised into six infantry divisions and a central body of army troops. The divisions were numbered in sequence (following behind the eight existing regular divisions but taking precedence over the territorial divisions) and were named after army regional commands. For example, twelve battalions drawn from Scottish regiments formed the 9th (Scottish) Division.

The new army was impressive enough on paper but in reality it was nothing more than a collection of raw recruits (the 'first hundred thousand' as they liked to call themselves) without uniforms or military equipment of any kind. More new armies were formed as recruits came streaming in. The second, authorised on 11 September 1914, was a mirror image of the first being made up, in the main, of the second service battalions of the same line regiments and bearing the same sequence of divisional names beginning with the 15th (Scottish) Division. A third was authorised two days later but as recruiting varied considerably from place to place the naming of divisions after army commands had to be abandoned. A fourth new army quickly followed, and then a fifth. In all, 30 infantry divisions were raised, every one of which served overseas, as the following table shows. The break in the sequence of divisional numbers reflects the formation, already described, of three additional regular divisions: the 27th, 28th and 29th.

New Army	Division	1st Theatre of War
1st (K1)	9th (Scottish)	France
	10th (Irish)	Gallipoli
	11th (Northern)	Gallipoli
	12th (Eastern)	France
	13th (Western)	Mediterranean
	14th (Light)	France
2nd (K2)	15th (Scottish)	France
	16th (Irish)	France
	17th (Northern)	France
	18th (Eastern)	France
	19th (Western)	France
	20th (Light)	France

3rd (K3)	21st	France
	22nd	France
	23rd	France
	24th	France
	25th	France
	26th	France
4th (K4)*	30th	France
	31st	France
	32nd	France
	33rd	France
	34th	France
	35th	France
5th (K5)*	36th (Ulster)	France
	37th	France
	38th (Welsh)	France
	39th	France
	40th	France
	41st	France

*Second formation. In April 1915 the divisions of the original fourth new army were broken up to provide reserves for the other new armies. The original fifth became the fourth, and a new fifth was added.

By the Spring of 1915, the British army had at its disposal 70 infantry divisions: 11 regular, 28 territorial, 30 new army, and one division (the Naval Division) raised by the Admiralty; the strength remained more or less at this level for the rest of the war.[19] The establishment of an infantry division at that time was just over 18,000 officers and men; 5,000 horses; 72 field guns in four artillery brigades of 18 guns each; and all supporting services including a supply train and ambulance brigades. There were also 500 bicycles and 34 cars. The infantry element, about 12,000 strong, consisted of 12 battalions (from various regiments) organised into three infantry brigades of four battalions each. A division was commanded by a major-general; each infantry brigade by a brigadier-general and a battalion - 1,000 men - by a lieutenant colonel. An infantry division on the march stretched some 15 miles along the road.[20]

The Welsh Army

In Wales, there was an even greater rush to arms than elsewhere, despite its history of radicalism and antipathy to military affairs. With a population of less than five per cent of that of Britain as a whole on which to draw, the three Welsh regiments of the line - the Royal Welsh Fusiliers, the South Wales Borderers and the Welsh Regiment - each with two regular battalions at the beginning of the war, supplied between them no less than 25 infantry battalions for the five new armies: seven per cent of the total.[21] In addition, these regiments provided territorial battalions for the Welsh Territorial Division (one of the original 14 territorial divisions in the pre-war British army) and for a 'second line' territorial division formed at the beginning of the war,[22] together with a number of pioneer (pick and shovel) battalions for the new armies, and numerous infantry battalions for the reserve. Nor was the contribution to the army by Wales confined to units bearing the name of the Principality. Welshmen also enlisted in large numbers in the various technical corps; in the Royal Artillery; and in those English regiments which had looked for some years to Wales for many of their recruits. About half the men of the Grenadier Guards, for example, was said to come from Wales.[23]

At first, Lloyd George took little interest in these military developments. Once the decision to enter the war had been taken, he busied himself almost exclusively with financial affairs, dealing first with a crisis of confidence in the City and then with longer-term problems at the Treasury.[24] Doubts about the extent of Britain's involvement in the war still plagued him. 'They are pressing the territorials to volunteer for the war,' he wrote to his wife on 11 August as the Expeditionary Force embarked for France. 'We mustn't do that just yet. We are keeping the seas for France - that ought to suffice here for the moment especially as we are sending 100,000 men to help her to bear the first brunt of the attack. This is all that counts for Russia will come in soon. I am dead against a war of conquest to crush Germany for the benefit of Russia. Beat the German Junker but no war on the German people etc. I am not going to sacrifice my nice little boy for that purpose. You must write Wil [his son, Gwilym] telling him on no account to be bullied into volunteering abroad.'[25]

Some weeks later, however, Lloyd George's mood changed and in September he seized an opportunity to demonstrate a new-found commitment to total war. This opportunity came when, towards the end of August, Lord Derby sought to help the hard-pressed War Office by offering to raise and organise local battalions in Liverpool and to administer them until the army was ready to take them over. The offer was eagerly accepted by the army and the idea soon spread. The cities of Liverpool and Manchester between them produced enough infantry for a complete division.[26] Local committees sprang up in other cities and towns to raise similar units and, by stimulating the idea of 'togetherness', they encouraged friends and acquaintances to join these 'Pals' battalions en masse. Most units of the fourth and fifth Kitchener armies were raised and provided for in this way. Politicians were pressed on to the recruitment platforms, Lloyd George among them. Before an audience of London Welshmen in the Queen's Hall, London on 19 September 1914 he delivered what has been described as one of the greatest and most inspired speeches of his career, one that was to influence his whole future and dramatically affect the pattern of recruiting in Wales. Roundly condemning the Prussian Junker, he said:

They think we cannot beat them. It will not be easy. It will be a long job. It will be a terrible war. But in the end we shall march through terror to triumph. We shall need all our qualities - every quality that Britain and its people possess - prudence in counsel, daring in action, tenacity in purpose, courage in defeat, moderation in victory...

And not content with the few 'Pals' battalions which had begun to be raised on local initiative in Wales, he called for a complete Welsh army. He appealed to 'little Wales' to continue to do her duty to 'little Belgium' and Russia's 'little brother' Serbia:

I should like to see a Welsh army in the field. I should like to see the race who faced the Normans for hundreds of years in their struggle for freedom, the race that helped to win the battle of Crecy, the race that fought for a generation against the greatest captain in Europe - I should like to see that race give a good taste of its quality in this struggle. And they are going to do it.[27]

Lloyd George, who had worried about the speech, thought the audience was strangely unresponsive, but the press went wild with enthusiasm. *The Times*, not normally well disposed towards Lloyd George, was ecstatic, much to Lloyd George's scornful amusement. Many of his colleagues thought it the best speech he had ever made and Sir Edward Grey is said to have wept when he read it.[28] This response greatly enhanced Lloyd George's prestige in the country and enabled him, among other things, to overcome Kitchener's known hostility to the creation of large all-Welsh (or all-Irish) military formations. Lloyd George raised the issue in Cabinet and won.[29] On 23 September the newspapers announced that the Secretary of State, Lord Kitchener, had 'given his sanction to the formation of a Welsh army corps, which was urged by Lloyd George in his speech on Saturday,' and that a provisional committee had been formed to carry out the project. Formal approval was given by the War Office a few weeks later.

The first, and only, task undertaken by the provisional committee was to arrange a 'representative National Conference of leading men' at the Park Hall, Cardiff on 29 September.[30] Lloyd George went down to raise support for what he now described, with greater precision, as a Welsh army corps of two divisions. He aimed high in quality as well as quantity. 'It is important,' he told his audience of Welsh peers, bishops, politicians, employers and trade unionists, 'we should secure the cream of the youth of this country for the purpose of this army...If we can only get the right type of young man to join we will have one of the most magnificent little armies ever turned out of this country. That is what we are aiming at.'[31]

The conference passed a resolution that Wales, including Monmouthshire, should become a military administrative area for the purpose of recruiting the necessary men and that 'the National Executive Committee to organise the Welsh army corps, and advise and direct it, be and is hereby appointed'.[32]

The reaction of the military authorities was understandably cool, much as they would welcome extra recruits. Army life is centred on the regiment: there is no tradition of loyalty to the army as such, only to the regiment and the Crown. The thought of a national army, particularly one raised by a politician - and a Welsh politician at that - naturally filled them with unease. The Cardiff *Western Mail* reported a Welsh officer 'of considerable experience' as saying that, as he understood the proposal, 'Mr Lloyd George is not seeking to raise a complete Welsh army corps in the strict military sense of the term, but to enlist between 40,000 and 50,000 additional men in Wales to supplement the large contribution which Wales has already made to the Army'. 'You must bear in mind,' the officer said, 'that in the regular army the best morale is the result of esprit de corps which exists in regard to the maintenance of the honour of the regiment to which the men belong.'[33] This is a curious interpretation to put on Lloyd George's speech which clearly referred to 'an army in the field' and not merely to a source of recruits to be distributed here and there as the occasion demanded. A similar misunderstanding of Lloyd George's intention was to be the cause of continuing friction between the General Officer Commanding-in-Chief, Western Command, and the Welsh army corps Executive Committee over the months ahead.

The Committee, however, was not short of support. A certain Captain Vaughan, for example, wanted to go beyond a purely fighting force. 'A corps of 40,000 men is a fine thing,' he wrote. 'A single regiment of a thousand men armed and equipped for war, is a far finer thing, for it would sweep the 40,000 out of existence in a single flash if the 40,000 were unarmed and unequipped...If we wanted to do a fine thing which will make our work to be of tenfold effect we must establish a Welsh Armament and Equipment Company (Limited) in order to arm and equip our men ready for action...'[34] Not surprisingly, this bizarre advice was completely ignored.

Unfortunately for the Executive Committee, there was no immediate rush of recruits to the new army corps. Lloyd George's appeal had in fact come almost too late. By the middle of September there had been clear signs that the recruitment boom was over, and the Executive Committee, for all its propaganda and publicity (which included a visit to Cardiff by the Prime Minister) found it hard to reverse the trend. Some began to worry that Wales' reputation might suffer. 'Wales has a right to feel aggrieved - if you could have grievances in face of the present crises,' said Sir Ivor Herbert in a recruiting speech for the Welsh army corps, '-that from the national point of view she had given generously from her manhood, in the mass of the British army, and that thereafter it might appear that Wales had really not done all she could have done, because there were thousands of Welshmen in regiments which had no connection whatever with their native land.[35] Later on, however, recruitment improved, stimulated partly by a special reduction of the minimum height requirement to 5ft 3ins in recognition of the small stature of Welshmen and the authorisation of 'bantam' battalions with a minimum height of 5ft, and partly by news of the fall of Antwerp to the Germans which brought the war close to the British coast. By the end of the year about 10,000 recruits had been found. Thereafter they came in at a rate of some 4,000 a month and by October 1915 the target of between 40,000 and 50,000 had been reached.[36]

Units of the Welsh Army Corps
Formal authority for the raising of the Welsh army corps by the Executive Committee had been given by the Army Council to the General Officer Commanding-in-Chief, Western Command on 10 October 1914, 'the units to be raised as Service battalions of the existing Welsh regular regiments'.[37] By this time, thanks to the initiative of local committees, some units were already taking shape. A 'Pals' battalion of the Royal Welsh Fusiliers formed at Rhyl and was up to strength by 2 October. A similar battalion of the Welsh Regiment, raised at Swansea, had recruited 347 men by 10 October and was therefore at one-third of full strenght. Another battalion of the Welsh Regiment, the 1st Rhondda, which formed on 1st October as a Kitchener third army battalion, was diverted to the Welsh army corps at the Executive Committee's request. At the end of October the Welsh army corps boasted four full battalions, the three mentioned above and a second from the Rhondda valley. By the end of the year this had increased to twelve battalions; enough to form the 1st Division:[38]

Battalion No.	Battalion Name	Source of recruits
13th RWF	1st North Wales	Rhyl and surroundings
14th RWF	Carnarvon and Anglesey	Llandudno and surroundings
15th RWF	London Welsh	Welshmen in London

16th RWF	2nd North Wales	'Overspill' from 13th RWF
10th Welsh	1st Rhondda	Rhondda valleys
13th Welsh	2nd Rhondda	Rhondda valleys
14th Welsh	Swansea	Swansea and district
15th Welsh	Carmarthenshire	Carmarthen and parts of Glamorgan
16th Welsh	Cardiff City	Cardiff and district
17th Welsh	Glamorgan	Men below normal minimum height in Glamorgan
10th SWB	1st Gwent	Coalfield and ironworks in Monmouthshire
11th SWB	2nd Gwent	Monmouthshire coalfield and Brecon

Shortly afterwards, the 17th Welsh was transferred to a 'bantam' brigade in another division and the 17th Battalion, the Royal Welsh Fusiliers, took its place in the 1st Division. This apart, the composition of the 1st Division, in terms of battalions, remained unchanged until the last year of the war.

On 18 November the Executive Committee announced the formation of the three infantry brigades of the 1st Division:

First Brigade (Brig.-Gen. Owen Thomas), based at Llandudno, consisting of the four battalions of the Royal Welsh Fusiliers (and known unofficially as the North Wales Brigade).

Second Brigade (Brig.-Gen. RHW Dunn), based at Rhyl, consisting of four battalions of the Welsh Regiment: the two Rhondda battalions, the Swansea battalion and the Carmarthen battalion.

Third Brigade (Brig.-Gen. Ivor Philipps), based at Colwyn Bay, consisting of the two battalions of the South Wales Borderers, the Cardiff City battalion of the Welsh Regiment and, until replaced by the 17th RWF, the Glamorgan 'bantam' battalion of the Welsh Regiment.[39]

Two of the brigadiers, Owen Thomas and Ivor Philipps MP, were founder members of the Executive Committee. The former, certainly, and the latter, probably, owed his new appointment to

Lloyd George. Frances Stevenson (Lloyd George's secretary and mistress) records a meeting at the War Office between Lloyd George and Kitchener during which Lloyd George said that he had learned the name of the man being put forward for appointment as general of the North Wales brigade and had doubts about his suitability for the post. 'K. agreed and asked C. [the Chancellor, Lloyd George] if he had anyone in mind. C. suggested Colonel O.T. and K. rather fell in with the idea. He asked where the colonel was, and when he heard he was in the building, sent for him and appointed him brigadier-general on the spot. C. said it was a most dramatic touch, and very magnanimous on K.'s part as he must have known that it was the colonel who had been supplying C. with complaints about the War Office and the Welsh army corps. C. was very pleased with the appointment. The new brigadier seemed dazed at the sudden elevation...'[40]

The evidence that Lloyd George had a direct hand in the appointment of Ivor Philipps as brigadier is less clear, though subsequent events leave little room for doubt. Within two months of the appointment, Ivor Philipps received a further promotion to major-general and was given command of the 1st Division of the Welsh army corps, an appointment for which he had been pressing. This was certainly Lloyd George's doing. 'I have seen Ivor Philipps and confirmed Gwilym's appointment with him if P. gets the generalship of the division,' he wrote to his wife. 'Have seen K. about that now and think it will be all right.'[41] Lloyd George's call for sacrifice by the youth of Wales does not seem to have been intended to embrace his son Gwilym, who was now assured of a safe and comfortable position as Ivor Philipps's aide-de-camp.

Ivor Philipps had been Liberal Member of Parliament for Southampton for the previous eight years. Even allowing for the acute shortage of experienced regular officers, it seems remarkable that a politician who had ended his military career in the Indian army as a relatively junior officer, more than ten years before the war, should receive such rapid promotion to high command. The appointment of Gwilym as his aide-de-camp could not have been a deciding factor in Philipps's first promotion - to brigade command - for the rank of brigadier carried no entitlement to personal staff. Even a manipulator as skilful as Lloyd George would not have given much for Gwilym's chances if two promotions for Philipps had to be secured to achieve it. A hint of another motive can however be found in an entry that Frances Stevenson made in her diary almost to the day on which Ivor Philipps took up his divisional command. She records that Lloyd George had mentioned to her a great kindness shown to him many years earlier by Ivor Philipps's elder brother, Lord St. Davids. At a time when Lloyd George's political and financial prospects were at a low ebb, Lord St. Davids had offered to lend him £500. 'C. was mightily touched,' Frances Stevenson wrote, 'for he said the man had nothing to gain from his generous offer then, nor could he know that C. would ever be in a position to repay him. But although C. did not accept the offer, yet he has never forgotten St. Davids's generosity, and St.D. will never ask him for anything in vain.'[42] Lloyd George's recalling of this earlier favour at a time when Ivor Philipps was moving upwards through the higher ranks, suggests that the two events were not unrelated. A word of support for Philipps from his brother would not have fallen on deaf ears.

The movement of units of the Welsh army corps to the coastal resorts of North Wales to form the three brigades began in December 1914. In London, the officers of the London Welsh battalion (the 15th RWF) were given a banquet to wish them 'God-speed'. Lloyd George found time to be present in spite of being heavily preoccupied with Cabinet business. He was, he said in proposing the toast, 'proud to be President of the battalion, and still more proud to find among the list of officers a young officer called Captain Richard Lloyd George'. He followed up this reference to his elder son with an expression of hope that 'there would soon be another Lloyd George among the lieutenants of the battalion,'[43] this being a reference to Gwilym, who transferred to the battalion a few weeks later, en route for Ivor Philipps's office.

On 31 December the citizens of Cardiff turned out 'in their thousands' to give a send off to the Cardiff City battalion which had broken its journey at Cardiff station on its way from Porthcawl to Colwyn Bay. The welcome at the end of the journey was equally enthusiastic. The Cardiff City battalion and the 1st Gwent were met at Colwyn Bay station by town dignitaries and the clergy and were given, according to the *Western Mail*, a 'hearty' reception. The town was gaily decorated in their honour although this was hardly noticed in the pouring rain. At all three resorts the growing army of men was comfortably billeted by the sea; hardly conducive to good training the officers thought, but much appreciated by the troops. 'We are in clover,' one of them said, 'and cannot wish for greater comfort.'[44]

After two months marching and drilling - mainly on the sea front before a crowd of interested spectators - the units acquired enough 'soldierly bearing' to make a full-scale review worthwhile. Lloyd George, accompanied by General Mackinnon, the GOC-in-C Western Command, inspected the North Wales brigade on 1 March, St David's day, and the other two brigades a day later. St David's day, according to the London *Daily News*, 'was marked by features distinctly expressive of what may be termed the new Welsh nationalism. The newly formed Welsh Guards mounted guard for the first time over the King at Buckingham Palace; Mr Lloyd George was present at a parade of the North Wales brigade at Llandudno and an address was presented to him at an eisteddfod in the evening; flags were sold in Wales and London on behalf of the national fund for Welsh troops, and the Welsh national emblem was flown over the Chancellor's residence in Downing Street.'[45] The correspondent of the Liverpool *Daily Post* was even more lyrical, presumably with the paper's North Wales readership in mind:

> Llandudno has today entertained the largest crowd of excursionists that has ever honoured the town with a visit in the winter season. They came, thousands upon thousands of them, men, women and children from all parts of North Wales, not attracted by the sea, though that was superlatively grand as it rolled in great billows on to the shore and here and there in angry spurts dashed over the promenade, but to take part in the first inspection of the First Brigade of the Welsh army corps, to lionise the Chancellor of the Exchequer, and to celebrate St David's day in an entirely new fashion.
>
> Early comers found the town thronged with visitors among whom sellers of miniature red dragon flags were doing a brisk trade for the benefit of the fund to provide comfort for Welsh soldiers. The four battalions comprising Brigadier-General Owen Thomas's command were drawn up on the wind-swept promenade, the whole length and width of which appeared to be carpeted with blue and khaki - the blue uniforms of the 'Pals' and the khaki of the three other

battalions including the stalwart London Welsh. Every man paid homage to St David by wearing in his cap or through his shoulder strap the leek of old Wales. The march past, first in column and afterwards in platoon formation, was splendidly done. The men were, of course, delighted to be on the move, and were aglow with the exercise, marching with a rhythmic swing and sure tread to their own excellent bands...[46]

Lloyd George was suitably impressed. 'One of the most magnificent spectacles I have ever seen,' he is reported as saying.[47] General Mackinnon was more cautious, though he professed to be pleased. 'There was a doubt in the minds of many whether a Welsh corps could be raised at all,' he said later that day, 'and whether if raised it could be efficient.' The reason for the first doubt, he added, was that they had been late in starting...Being so late in the field it was very difficult for them to get instructors, but the proof of the pudding, he said, would be in the eating, and he congratulated the commanding officers on what he had seen that morning. He was sure that 'with the additional training which the officers could give the men they would soon be worthy to take their places by the side of His Majesty's regular army'.[48]

Around this time, other divisional troops were building up to full strength. Two artillery brigades of four batteries each were based at Pwllheli; another at Criccieth and a fourth at Portmadoc - all 40 to 50 miles away by road from the divisional headquarters at Colwyn Bay. They had no guns, but practised limbering up using pairs of old bus wheels fastened to long poles. Also in the Pwllheli/Portmadoc area were four companies of troops forming the divisional supply train, and three field ambulance units, although the latter moved up to Prestatyn, and nearer to the infantry, in early March. Three field companies of engineers were even further away, at Abergavenny, in the border country of South Wales.[49]

But even as Lloyd George was enjoying his moment of minor triumph reviewing the infantry in North Wales, the writing for the army corps was on the wall. By the end of February it appeared to the Executive Committee that it would be difficult to complete the second division unless there was greater coordination of recruiting in Wales for the regular army, the territorials and the Welsh army corps, and unless there was a concerted effort to get into much closer contact with the sources of recruits. The Committee therefore proposed to General Mackinnon that strong recruiting agencies should be established in each Welsh county and that attempts should be made to work out, in conjunction with the local employers, quotas for each county of men who could be drawn into military service without injury to the industrial effort.[50] This imaginative proposal for the best use of manpower - which anticipated the official scheme for national registration - drew a sharp response from the General Officer Commanding-in-Chief, in which he gave vent to his true feelings about the Welsh army corps:

> At present the Welsh army corps is looked upon as a unit and apart from any other Welsh troops, and orders have been given that all men who enlist in Wales are to go to the 43rd Division [then the official army designation for the 1st Division of the Welsh army corps] in preference to [other] Service battalions. Pals battalions have been raised; the men are billeted in popular seaside resorts, and the Welsh army corps has been boomed by some of the most influential gentlemen of Wales, and last and by no means least, has had the personal advocacy of the Chancellor of the Exchequer.

This outburst reflected Mackinnon's concern at the increasing difficulty of maintaining the special reserve battalions which served the Welsh regular battalions already fighting overseas. These were being starved of recruits by the expanding Welsh army corps and, with growing losses at the front, something needed to be done. He therefore proposed that all recruits enlisted for the Royal Welsh Fusiliers, the South Wales Borderers, and the Welsh Regiment should be sent to the special reserve battalions of the regiments to be drafted by the military authorities 'where their services are most required'.[51]

At first, the Committee resisted, holding firmly to the view that there would be a marked falling off in recruits if the idea of a second division were to be abandoned. By July, however, the Committee was having second thoughts and decided to submit to a decision by the Army Council. Two months later, on 27 October 1915, the Committee assembled in London to hear the Army Coucil's verdict relayed by Lord Derby. In the words of the

Committee's report: 'His Lordship stated that the War Office view was that new units were not then desirable, and that every effort was necessary for the recruitment of reserves. With that declaration, which the Committee accepted, recruiting for the Welsh army corps was brought to an end.'[52]

Ironically, this decision came at a time when the original recruiting target of between 40,000 and 50,000 men had been achieved. The 1st Division (by this time officially renumbered the 38th (Welsh) Division and in the 5th New Army) was fully up to strength and receiving final training in the south of England in preparation for its move to France. Seven other battalions had been formed, including a complete brigade of four 'bantam' battalions which was later transferred to the 40th Division as the Welsh Bantam Brigade. The three other battalions passed to the reserve.

Thus Lloyd George's dream of an army corps of two divisions just failed to come true. If he had launched his campaign a few weeks earlier, when recruiting was at its height, the result might have been otherwise, although, of course, at the expense of other Kitchener armies. Still, the creation of a complete division was in itself no mean achievement, and with its descriptive title and all Welsh make-up, the 38th (Welsh) Division carried with it something of the aura of Lloyd George's 'Welsh Army'. Whether, as Lloyd George had hoped, it would be 'one of the most magnificent little armies ever turned out' remained to be seen.

Training

In the opening months of the war, the army faced the enormous task of training and supplying the vast new army of recruits, to bring it up to something like the pitch of the highly trained armies of the continental powers. Kitchener's critics maintained that it could not be done in time to affect the course of the war, pointing out that in peacetime, when the army had little else to do, it took a year of hard training to turn a new recruit into an effective soldier. Now the army was fighting the greatest war of all time and recruits were pouring in at well over a hundred times the peacetime rate. Even those most closely involved found it a daunting experience. 'I was shocked by my first contact with the new army,' Guy Chapman wrote later. 'It was not so much the circumstances; the dull little south coast watering-place in winter; the derelict palazzo, the headquarters facing on one side the tumbling grey sea and on the other an unkempt field; it was not the men in shabby blue clothes and forage caps with their equipment girt about them with bits of string; it was the obvious incapacity and amateurishness of the whole outfit which depressed.'[53]

The most immediate problem was the shortage of experienced officers. Regular officers on leave from India were diverted at once to the new armies and some others were kept back from the Expeditionary Force itself, but these were nothing like enough for the task. The first new Kitchener army did reasonably well in getting about six serving regular officers in each battalion but the subsequent armies were lucky to have even one. The growing units of the 38th (Welsh) Division were no exception, and in common with other locally raised units of the fourth and fifth new armies, had to resort largely to the use of 'dug-outs' - retired ex-regular officers - and part-time soldiers of the old militia, though eventually the commanding officers of some battalions came from the Indian Army. The division also had more than its fair share of Liberal Members of Parliament: Ivor Philipps in command of the division; Hamar Greenwood, a Canadian of Welsh descent who had settled in Britain (and who later became Chief Secretary for Ireland in Lloyd George's post-war administration and, later still, as Lord Greenwood, Chairman of the Conservative Party) in command of the 10th South Wales Borderers; and David Davies, later Lord Davies of Llandinam, a wealthy coal-owner and industrialist, in command of the 14th Royal Welsh Fusiliers. Although Hamar Greenwood was not a member, all three attended meetings of the Welsh army corps Executive Committee which was influential in filling senior posts. 'You will be glad to hear that...I have recommended the appointment of Major V Paget (retired RHA) for the command of the 1st Division Field Artillery,' the chairman of the Committee, Lord Plymouth, wrote to Lloyd George at one point. '...Major Paget is my brother-in-law.'[54]

Almost all the junior officers were new to the army although some had received rudimentary training in the officer cadet corps which had been introduced into universities and public schools by Haldane in 1908. It was mainly on these junior officers and on the non-commissioned officers that the burden of training fell. As far as possible, the non-commissioned officers

were drawn from among reservists and re-enlisted men, thereby
providing the experience much needed in these ranks. To increase
their numbers, the War Office raised the upper age limit for
re-enlistment to fifty[55] but even this failed to meet the
demand and many promotions had to be made from among the raw
recruits. One new recruit to the Swansea battalion, who had had
some drill instruction in the police service before joining the
army, later recalled being sent to Aldershot on a short
intensive course of physical training and bayonet fighting. On
his return to the battalion he was immediately promoted to the
rank of sergeant and given the task of imparting to the new
recruits all that he had learned.[56]

Uniforms and rifles were in short supply while industry
geared itself up to meet the enormous increase in demand. Most
of the Kitchener armies made do with 'horrible blue serge
uniforms impossible to smarten up save by brass
buttons',[57] but for some units of the Welsh division the
Executive Committee provided uniforms of brethyn-llwyd (a
hard-wearing brown Welsh cloth) which were fairly smart and
therefore popular. Rifles remained scarce however for more than
a year except for antiquated (and condemned) models suitable
only for drill purposes. There was also a shortage of most other
equipment and this severely limited the training programme. But
in spite of the difficulties, the want of equipment, and the
obvious lack of professionalism at all levels, the men were keen
to learn. 'Friday was a very bad day for drilling or any outdoor
exercising for the men of Cardiff City battalion at Porthcawl,'
reported the *Western Mail* on 5 December 1914. 'From early
morning there were gales and heavy downfalls of rain that would
drench one to the skin. The men have been in some cases drilled
in small companies in the shelter of high walls.'

With the move to North Wales, platoon drill and other platoon
and company training began in earnest. 'At the height of
drilling time it is a great sight on the "front" and one which
attracts a large number of townspeople to watch the evolution,'
said one newspaper report. 'At one point the elementary stages
of "forming fours" etc are in progress under the direction of
one of the most exacting of instructors. In another position,
squads are being instructed in the mysteries of Swedish drill.
Again one comes across a group of men being put through a course
of signalling and at other points various other exercises are

being carried out.'[58]

Arms drill and bayonet practice followed. Some instruction was also given in the theory of musketry (rifle shooting), although firing practice itself had to be deferred until suitable rifles were available. There was also plenty of route marching, so much so that in April 1915 the Cardiff City battalion, reporting a shortage of socks, blamed this on the amount of marching done by the battalion. Sometimes there would be mock battles at company or battalion strength, in which a small force would be sent off in advance to take up defensive positions and scouts sent out to find them. A dummy attack would follow. On 15 December 1914, C Company of the London Welsh battalion defended the rocky outcrop of the Little Orme at Llandudno against two other companies of the battalion which had been ordered to attack that position. 'The men embarked upon their task with enthusiasm and negotiated many difficult obstacles in their endeavour to gain the heights,' reported the *Western Mail* with the exaggerated enthusiasm characteristic of most newspaper reports of the time. 'Colonel Fox-Pitt, the commanding officer, who acted as umpire, was loud in his praise of the way the men had carried out the operations, especially the way they took cover.'[59]

But these high jinks fell a long way short of the preparation needed for large-scale war, and the disadvantage of having the troops scattered across Wales soon became evident. Brigade training was difficult enough while the men were still in billets, but divisional manoeuvres were almost impossible, although in May all three brigades did manage to get together for a day's exercise in the hills south of Colwyn Bay. 'Each man took his day's rations,' said the *Carnarvon Herald* on 14 May, 'and the day in the hills, thanks to glorious weather was enjoyed both as an outing and as a sound lesson of real practical value.' By then, there was talk of a move to the army training grounds in the south of England, but this had to be delayed until the camps there had been vacated by the first and second new armies. These divisions began to move to France in July and by the end of August all units of the 38th (Welsh) Division were gathered together in the Winchester area where more advanced brigade and divisional training could begin.

The shortage of rifles persisted until November, when the division was told to prepare to move to France. In the last few,

frantic weeks before embarkation each man was put through a
hurried course on the rifle ranges on Salisbury Plain[60]
and were pronounced proficient in the firing of arms. The
artillery was less fortunate and had to delay its departure for
France for a few weeks in order to get in its first practice
firings with live ammunition.

During these final stages of preparation, younger, more
experienced officers - including some who had been wounded at
the front and since recovered, and others from service in India
- took over many of the brigade and battalion commands. A young
37 year-old brigadier, L A E Price-Davies, who had won the
Victoria Cross in South Africa, replaced Owen Thomas as
commander of the 1st Brigade (now renumbered the 113th) and
another regular officer, T O Marden, who had commanded the
1st Battalion of the Welsh Regiment in France, took over the
2nd Brigade (now the 114th) from Brig.-Gen. Dunn. The old
3rd Brigade (which became the 115th) however remained under the
command of Horatio Evans who had been promoted from command of
the 4th District, Western Command, to succeed Ivor Philipps when
the latter had taken over the whole division. Evans was 55 years
of age, which was rather old for a brigadier going on active
service, but a lively mind and long experience of fighting in
South Africa and on the North West frontier of India no doubt
counted in his favour. Owen Thomas was bitterly disappointed to
learn that he would not be taking his brigade to France though
he brightened up on receiving a complimentary letter from Lloyd
George which, he said, would save him from being 'openly cursed'
by fellow countrymen for having broken faith with the hundreds
of parents whom he had influenced to send their sons with him to
the front.[61]

One Sunday at the end of November a special correspondent of
the *Manchester Guardian* motored through the frost-bound
countryside, 'visiting the camps of Welsh soldiers scattered
about the slopes of the wooded Hampshire hills':

My mission was to find the Cymanfa, the big farewell drumhead
service, which, according to rumour, was to bring the men of
Wales together in the presence of Mr Lloyd George, the
creator of the Welsh army corps. There was no Cymanfa to be
discovered anywhere in the shivering encampments. Amiable
colonels said they had never heard of it or that they were

far too busy, and one even asked me to spell it...The Welsh soldiers are indeed far too furiously busy just now for Cymanfas. Preparations are going on for the great review tomorrow which will be the crown of many months of hard training and endurance cheerfully borne. Within a year the army has been welded into the splendidly efficient instrument it is today...

The Welshmen bring with them into their lonely exile a certain homely warmth and clannishness which you do not find in communities more racially mixed. To feel how the Welsh bring their own atmosphere with them into an alien land you must be there as I was, when the weary route-marchers swing back to camp, in the twilight singing 'Sospan Bach' which may be called the football national anthem of Wales and which has been heard on many a field of triumph.[62]

The division was to carry this peculiarly Welsh 'atmosphere' with it to the war in France. Wyn Griffith, an officer in the 15th Royal Welsh Fusiliers, has recorded a moment when one company was waiting to go up to the trenches on relief. 'They start singing in harmony...a fine old Welsh hymn in a minor key. The brigadier-general asks me, "Why do they always sing these mournful hymns? Most depressing - bad for morale. Why can't they sing something cheerful, like other battalions?" I try to explain to him that what they are singing now is what they sang as children, as I did, in chapel, in the world to which they really belong. They are being themselves, not men in uniform. They are back at home, with their families, in their villages. But he does not understand. Nor can he, with his background. I do not think I "understand" it myself; but the facts were there, and they still are. While they sang, they, and I, were in another country.'[63]

The correspondent of the *Manchester Guardian* had to admit that Lloyd George did not after all turn up to bid farewell to the Welsh division at Winchester although his daughter, Olwyn, was there, seeing off her two brothers. The preparations he had witnessed were for a review by the Queen, who, on Monday 29 November 1915, drove past in the pouring rain - an inspection which signalled the imminent departure of the division for France. What shape was it in, as it prepared to embark? The War Office, concious of the late start which the division had made and of the number of inexperienced civilians and 'aged dug-outs' among the officers originally appointed by Lloyd George and the Executive Committee, thought it a little less efficient than other divisions similarly bound for the Continent and wrote to the Commander-in-Chief in France suggesting further training if the position at the front line made this possible.[64] The troops however were full of confidence. One participant, recalling the occasion years afterwards, had this to say:

> On the whole, training turned us into a fairly smart, well disciplined and efficient force; morale was good, but I realised later that the training we received was related more to earlier wars, such as the South African campaign, than to the one in which we were about to be engaged.[65]

2. France, December 1915 - June 1916

You can hear the silence of it:
you can hear the rat of no-man's-land

Early on the morning of 1 December 1915, the leading battalions
of the 38th (Welsh) Division marched through Winchester en route
for Southampton, Le Havre and the British Expeditionary Force in
France, the rest of the division, less artillery, following
closely behind. They marched 'in an even drive of wind and rain,
into a late afternoon that found us on a wet quayside, staring
at a grey ship on a grey sea. Rain in England, rain in the
Channel and rain in France; mud on the Hampshire Downs and mud
in the unfinished horse-standings in Havre where we sheltered
from the rain during hours of waiting for a train.'[1] On
the outskirts of Southampton the bedraggled troops had made an
attempt to smarten themselves up and the bands played bravely as
they marched through the streets towards the docks. They need
not have bothered: after 16 months of war the sight of troops
marching through the port had become so familiar to the
inhabitants that nobody took any notice.[2] But in spite of
foul weather and rough seas, there was no mishap and by
6 December 1915, 526 officers; 15,447 other ranks; 1,580 horses
and mules; 526 horse-drawn vehicles; 515 bicycles; 70 lorries;
36 cars; 29 motor cycles and other paraphernalia of the division
were safely delivered to a billeting area 10 miles south of
St. Omer and about 30 miles behind the British front
line.[3] Here they joined the XI Corps in the centre of the
British First Army.

They moved at a time when the British supreme command, both
civil and military, was in disarray and British strategy in
turmoil. 1915 had been a year of failures, principally in the
Dardanelles where an attempt to capture the Gallipoli peninsula
had ended in disaster, but also on the Western Front,
particularly at Loos in September. Field Marshal Sir John
French, Commander-in-Chief of the British armies in France, was

in disgrace for mishandling the battle and for allegedly falsifying his dispatches. On 19 December he was recalled to England and replaced by General Sir Douglas Haig, commander of the First Army, who was told by Kitchener to 'keep friendly with the French' and look upon General Joffre 'as the C-in-C in France, where he knew the country and the general situation well.'[4]

Kitchener himself, however, was in difficulties. He had lost the confidence of his Ministerial colleagues on the War Committee who increasingly resented his autocratic and secretive ways - with some justification - and who now regarded him as a bad administrator.[5] Lloyd George angled for his dismissal on the grounds that he had given the Cabinet wrong advice about the Balkans and had so mismanaged the munitions problem that failure on the Western Front had been inevitable; but Kitchener was still popular in the country and Asquith, now heading a shaky coalition Government, could hardly take this step without risking his own position as Prime Minister. Instead he prevailed upon Kitchener to allow the Chief of the Imperial General Staff (CIGS) to take his place as the Government's chief adviser on strategy and suggested the appointment of Sir William ('Wully') Robertson - French's Chief of Staff in France - to the post of CIGS.[6] Robertson himself was encouraged to dictate his own terms before accepting office.[7] This he did to such effect that when he took up his appointment on 23 December Kitchener was reduced to a mere figurehead, responsible mainly for recruiting, clothing and feeding the army.

Although military operations in 1915 had ended in failure, the outlook was not entirely gloomy, if only because Britain's military strength was increasing rapidly with every day that passed:

> Like Pilgrim relieved of his burden, the nation, freed from the incubus of the Dardanelles, entered on the year 1916 on a note of hope. The new armies were rapidly putting on final touches and preparing to take the field. Many divisions had already been in action and behaved creditably. Others were fully prepared to outshine them. All over the country new munitions factories were sprouting up like mushrooms. Before the year was half spent what seemed an inexhaustable supply of heavy guns, light guns, machine guns and munitions of all kinds would be pouring into the various theatres of war.[8]

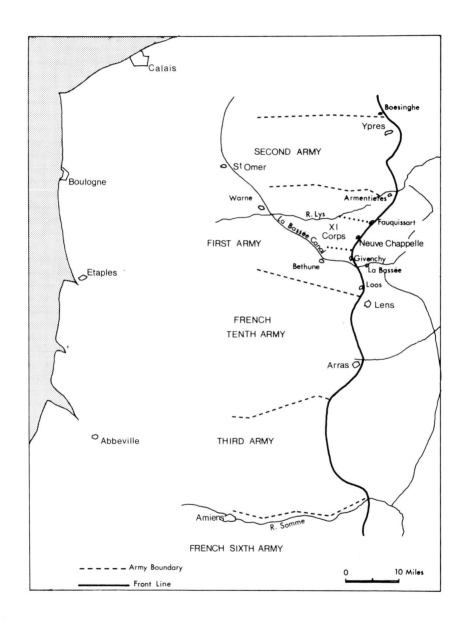

Map 1. The Western Front, December 1915.

Both Robertson and Haig were confirmed 'Westerners' believing that the Germans could be beaten only in France. All other theatres of war were therefore to be subordinated to the Western Front. During 1915, the British Expeditionary Force in France and Flanders had grown from 10 divisions to 37 (including two from Canada),[9] organised in three armies: two (the First and Second) holding a continuous line from Boesinghe in Belgium, to Loos in the coal fields of Northern France, and a third (the Third Army) sandwiched between the French Sixth and Tenth Armies in an area north of the River Somme (see map 1). Robertson was determined that as many divisions as possible should be released from Britain to serve in France and that they should be joined by troops from the Dardanelles. To this end, he moved quickly to discontinue all engagements on the Gallipoli peninsula. The Cabinet, after wrestling with the problem for weeks, had already decided on 27 December that the beachhead at Suvla and Anzec should be evacuated but that Cape Helles, the southernmost tip of the peninsula, should be retained. Robertson would have none of this and orded complete evacuation. He also instructed Murray, the army commander in Egypt, to reorganise the troops which were pouring into Egypt from Gallipoli and transfer them to France. Within six months, nine of the best divisions in Egypt had been sent to France.[10]

On 28 December 1915 the War Committee accepted 'in principle' that British forces should be concentrated on the Western Front and that preparations should be made for a major Franco/British offensive in the Spring to be carried out simultaneously with offensives on the Russian and Italian fronts - as had been recommended by an allied military conference at Chantilly on 8 December. Some members of the Committee had serious misgivings and the War Committee made it clear that their assent should not be 'construed as an authority for undertaking the offensive'.[11] In spite of this reservation, Robertson was well pleased and wrote immediately to tell Haig the good news. On 13 January, however, he had to write again, to say that the decision had been further watered down by the Cabinet:

There is a fairly strong party in the Cabinet opposed to offensive operations on your front in the Spring or indeed at any time. One wants to go to the Balkans, another to Baghdad, and another to allow the Germans to attack us. I have used all the arguments you or any other soldier would use, but not with complete success. In the War Committee decision I sent you a few days ago you will see that we are to make every effort 'to prepare' for offensive operations in the Spring. In the original draft I put we were to make every effort to 'undertake' offensive operations in the Spring. By a decision made today (which I will send you later) it has now been watered down to the effect that we are to 'prepare' for offensive operations in the Spring 'but without committing ourselves definitely to them'...[some] people are trying to get their way by urging us to wait for an offensive until we are at full strength, which they say will not be until well on in the Summer and amongst these people is Lloyd George who has received the Prime Minister's sanction to meet the French munitions and artillery authorities in France to discuss with them how much ammunition they think they will want before they can be ready and how long it will take them to get it. This is the thin end of the wedge for deferring matters.[12]

But whatever disagreement there might have been about the date of the coming offensive, the die was cast. 'Once authority was given to concentrate our maximum strength on the Western front' to quote Lord Hankey, 'it was inevitable that the generals would lose no time in setting to work. Very soon our available resources would be irretrievably committed to and locked up in that theatre. When the French, Italians and Russians were all attacking on their respective fronts it would have been morally impossible for the British Supreme Command to refuse the co-operation of the forces at their disposal in accordance with the plans of the Allied generals.'[13] In 1916 then, the weight of Kitchener's armies was to be thrown against the Germans; and they would fight on the Western Front. It was against this background that the 38th (Welsh) Division, with many others, moved to France.

Apprenticeship in the line

The strength of the XI Corps when the 38th Division joined it in December 1915 was three divisions: two in the front line and one in reserve. The Guards Division held the left sectors of the corps front north of Neuve Chapelle, and a new army division - the 19th (Western) - held the right sectors south of the village. The 46th (North Midland) Division, a territorial unit, was in reserve at St. Venant having come out of the line a few days before the arrival of the 38th. The 46th Division was destined to move, against the general flow, from the Western Front to Egypt as soon as the 38th had gained sufficient experience to take its place.[14] For the first four weeks in France, the 38th Division trained continuously for this role, both in and out of the line:

> They did short route marches each day along winding ways saturated with continued rain. They did platoon-drill and arm-drill in soggy fields behind their billets.
>
> They were given lectures on very wet days in the barn... lectures on military tactics that would be more or less commonly understood. Lectures on hygiene by the medical officer, who was popular, who glossed his technical discourses with every lewdness...
>
> One day the Adjutant addressed them on the history of the Regiment. Lectures by the Bombing Officer: he sat in the straw, a mild young man, who told them lightly of the efficacy of his trade; he predicted an important future for the new Mills Mk.IV grenade, just on the market; he discussed the improvised jam-tins of the veterans, of the bombs of after the Marne, grenades of Loos and Laventie - he compared these elementary, amateurish, inefficiencies with the compact and supremely satisfactory invention of this Mr Mills, to whom his country was so greatly indebted.
>
> He took the names of all those men professing efficiency on the cricket field - more particularly those who claimed to bowl effectively - and brushing away with his hand pieces of straw from his breeches, he sauntered off with his sections of grenades and fuses and explanatory diagrams of their mechanism stuffed into the pockets of his raincoat, like a departing commercial traveller.[15]

Bombing practice soon followed, at which most men threw at least one live bomb, and those selected to be bombers threw ten or more. Faulty grenades and occasional carelessness in handling made this a hazardous exercise in which a number of officers and men were killed, and others wounded. On the rifle ranges, the most accurate shots were trained as snipers, while the rest practised to bring their rate of fire up to 15 aimed rounds a minute - a fairly respectable rate, even if well short of the 30 rounds a minute claimed to have been achieved by the best of the regulars in the pre-war army. The troops also learned the basics of field engineering; how to revet earthworks with sandbags and timber; how to drain and pump; how to construct new traverses and dugouts. Machine gun crews fired live ammunition for the first time and elementary training was given in gas warfare, all officers and men passing through a tunnel of gas wearing the primitive gas helmets of the time.[16]

Between 10 December 1915 and 6 January 1916, battalions of the division were attached in turn to units of the two divisions in the front line to learn at first hand the business of trench warfare.[17] Wyn Griffith recalled his own feelings as he faced this initiation into the brotherhood of the trenches:

> Less than twenty-four hours stood between us and the trenches; there were two kinds of men in the world - those who had been in the trenches and the rest. We were to graduate from the one class to the other, to be reborn into the old age and experience of the front line, by the traversing of two miles over the fields of Flanders.[18]

The journey itself, across the churned-up, waterlogged valley of the River Lys, brought its own unpleasant experiences; unwelcome encounters with rotting corpses, huge rats and ice-cold water:

> Appear more Lazarus figures, where water gleamed between dilapidated breastworks, blue slime coated, ladling with wooden ladles; rising, bending, at their trenches dredging. They speak low. Cold gurgling followed their labours. They lift things, and a bundle-thing out; its shapelessness sags. From this muck-raking are singular stenches, long decay leavened; compounding this clay with that more precious, patient of baptism; chemical-corrupted once-bodies...
>
> You step down between inward inclining, heavy bulged, walls of earth; you feel the lateral slats firm foothold. Squeaking, bead-eyed hastening, many footed hurrying, accompanying each going forward.
>
> Break in the boards - pass it back
>
> The fluid mud is icily discomforting that circles your thighs...

By contrast, the front line with its signs of homeliness, of a culture 'already developed, already venerable and rooted' was almost welcome:

> You turn sharp left; the space of darkness about you seems of a different shape and character; earth walls elbow at you in a more complicated way. You stand fast against the parados.
>
>   And you too are assimilated, you too are of this people...[19]

The troops soon became absorbed in the dull routine of trench life: stand-to at dawn and dusk in case the enemy attacked in the half light, and at other times repairing trench walls, renewing barbed-wire, carrying stores and ammunition, and 'scheming against the insidious attack of water'.[20] This work was mainly carried out at night:

> Most of the daytime - invariably in the morning - the three lines, firing, support and reserve, were deserted except for a few sentries leaning against the parapet with periscopes handy, and for a sniper or two; everyone else was under cover, silent and, if possible, asleep. At dark a whole population suddenly appeared, literally out of the earth; working parties would set about draining, digging and wiring; from the rear, along the communication trenches, would come parties carrying rations, water, ammunition, sandbags, duck-boards, and everything imaginable. Behind these again the roads were packed with horsed wagons and limbers...Then dawn would approach, the trench garrison would stand to arms and be dismissed to begin another similar day.[21]

On Christmas Eve, the divisional artillery began to arrive from England and by 27 December the division was at last complete. At about the same time, the 46th Division departed leaving the 38th (Welsh) Division as corps reserve. By 6 January, the training programme was over and two complete brigades - the 113th and 114th - moved into the line to relieve a brigade each of the Guards and 19th Divisions, still under the eyes of experienced divisional commanders, but responsible, for the first time, for whole sectors of the front line system. On 12 January, the 113th

Brigade had its first break with routine, making a demonstration with 200 plywood dummy soldiers 'as if getting over the parapet'.[22] It repeated this ruse three times to represent three waves of infantry, while the artillery heavily shelled the German front line in the hope that the German infantry would have left their dug-outs to defend it. 'From the increase in rifle fire, it appears he reinforced his front line', wrote the XI Corps diarist, anxious to attribute a measure of success to this elementary piece of deception.

A few days later, the corps commander, Lt.-Gen. R Haking, satisfied with the division's progress, ordered Maj.-Gen. Philipps to prepare to take over the line from 19th Division with these words of approbation:

> Now that the 38th Division has completed its training in the trenches, and is about to take over half the front occupied by XI Corps, I wish to convey to all ranks my appreciation of the manner in which they have set to work to make themselves efficient...
>
> Although, of course, a good deal remains yet to be done, this division has made more rapid strides towards efficiency than any of the several new formations that I have had under my command during the campaign.
>
> Now that you are about to take over part of our line I anticipate with confidence that you will dominate the enemy in front of you; that your offensive spirit will be far superior to his; that your patrolling, sniping, trench mortar, bombing, infantry, artillery and engineer work will be better than his, and that with careful reconnaissance work and preparation you will shortly be able to continue the raids on his trenches which have already been carried out with such success by other divisions of the corps.[23]

This emphasis on ascendancy, on 'dominating the enemy in front', was common to most corps and army commanders at that time, but General Haking - whose penchant for offensive action was to cause unnecessary slaughter on this front some months later[24] - was a particularly enthusiastic proponent. The theme recurs time and time again in the records of his frequent conferences with his divisional commanders, as being the most effective way of 'breaking the enemy's morale'. Junior officers were sceptical and wondered if the losses were justified. The

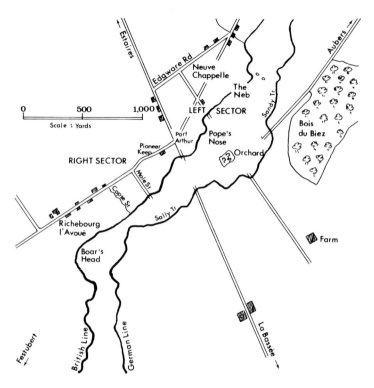

Map 2. 38th Division Sectors, 29 January 1916.

troops had few illusions, preferring, like the Germans and the French, a quiet life. The whole philosophy became something of a joke amongst them. Thus David Jones's ironic description of the chaos that ensues when, unwittingly, a party of Royal Welsh Fusiliers runs into a German patrol at night:

> The thudding and breath to breath you don't know which way, what way, you count eight of him in a flare-space, you can't find the lane [ie the gap in the wire] - the one way - you rabbit to and fro, you could cry...
> We maintain ascendancy in no-man's-land.[25]

At this time, however, there was a need to conserve ammunition for the coming offensive and extravagant raids and bombardments were discouraged. The line settled into a quiet routine of sporadic gun fire by day and reconnaissance patrols by night, perhaps two or three on each divisional front. 'Nothing to report', is a frequent entry in the 38th Division's diary. The following extract from a 38th Division tactical progress report describes a typical day in January 1916.[26] Map 2 shows the area to which the report refers.

Tactical Progress Report No.7
Right Sector
In the fog, this morning, two Germans were seen approaching one of our posts in the right sub-sector. The post with considerable restraint lay low, and 'Hands upped' the Germans when they were within 30 yards. From reports at present to hand, it would appear that these men belonged to the 55th Guard Reserve Regiment...

A listening post at Boar's Head located enemy's working party half way across no-man's land...Yesterday morning at 'stand-to' the Germans opposite Copse St. - Mole St. were heard to shout several times 'Who are you' while those further on our right shouted 'You bloody murderers'. This is eminently satisfactory if it indicates that our activity has been giving them a thin time...The machine gun mentioned in yesterday's report to be firing from the high breastwork behind Boar's Head did not reply to the fire of our machine guns for the first time. An officer was observed through a telescope to come up and speak to a man near point 95 [unidentifiable on trench map]. This officer wore a coat closed up at the throat and had a high straight collar. His cap was shaped like ours, and was blue in colour with a red band round it. His face seemed very pale but he looked particularly clean.

Left Sector
A searchlight which we attempted to use on the Orchard did not prove a success, the beam not being apparently powerful enough. Strong wire is reported [south of the Orchard]: two whistles were heard playing in the German lines. 'I've got my eye on you' appeared to be the tune. An officer's patrol from The Neb saw no sign of enemy work, but a strong enemy patrol was seen. Mining is suspected near The Neb, the men reporting the noise being experienced miners. Necessary precautions have been taken and investigations are being made. Opposite the right sub-sector, Left Sector, the enemy

appears to occupy an old communication trench in no-man's-land as Very lights were seen coming from it. Opposite the left sub-sector, the enemy were laughing and talking and playing mouth organs during the early part of the night. An officer's patrol from The Neb followed the willows to the wire near the German trenches. They heard talking and posts being hammered in, apparently in front of the parapet for wiring. On receipt of the patrol's report, machine gun fire was opened on the spot.

But although the front line was quiet, it was not without its hazards. Snipers' bullets and bursting shells on the one hand, and continual exposure to mud and water on the other, took a steady toll. During March and April, the Swansea battalion alone drafted in 100 officers and men a month, equivalent to more than 1,000 a month for the whole division.[27] On 17 May, the division lost one of its most senior officers. Lt.Col. F Gaskell, commanding officer of the 16th Welsh which he himself had raised at Cardiff, was mortally wounded when visiting his men at a crater in no-man's-land. His second in command, Major Frank Smith took over the battalion.

In mid-February, the Guards Division transferred to the Second Army. The 19th Division replaced it in the line and the 35th Division joined the corps to bring it up to strength. At the same time, the whole corps moved sideways to the south and the 38th (Welsh) Division took over at Festubert, where for a while it had three brigades in the line together. At Festubert the ground was low lying and completely waterlogged. The front line consisted of a series of isolated posts called 'islands', each held by a garrison of from 10 to 20 men. These posts were all that remained of a once continuous front line which elsewhere had been washed away. On the islands themselves the parapets were barely bullet-proof and dug-out accommodation was almost non-existent. Communication trenches were flooded and the islands could only be reached across open ground. As the German front line was only 200 yards away, and on slightly higher ground, the islands were unapproachable by day. 100 yards behind the islands was a rudimentary support trench, again barely habitable, and further back the old British line of 1915, where most of the front line fighters were garrisoned, though even this was broken down in places and sadly lacking in dug-outs. In these miserable conditions, the Welsh Division spent most of its time draining the land and improving the defences. There was little time for fighting.

A few weeks later, however, the corps absorbed the 33rd Division, extending its frontage further southward to Cuinchy and Auchy beyond the La Bassee Canal, and the 38th Division again shuffled south, exchanging the watery wastes of Festubert for slightly drier, but less restful surroundings at Givenchy. Givenchy was notorious as an area which was actively mined by the Germans:

> A mile to the north stood Festubert, where men fought more with water than with fellow men; a mile or two to the south the trenches were dry, but on Givenchy hill there was no respite from fire or flood, nor from that devil's volcano of a sprung mine. To stand in the trench was to wait to be blown up, without warning, from below, or to be struck down by some terror from the sky in the shape of a bomb, grenade or shell.[28]

The activity was not, however, all one-sided and at his conference on 8 March the corps commander gave the division his greatest accolade: he congratulated it for gaining 'ascendency' over the enemy through its activities on the Givenchy front.

At the end of March, the 39th Division, newly arrived from England, joined the XI Corps for training, bringing its total strength up to five divisions, all new army, reflecting the preponderence of new army divisions on the Western Front at that time. The diagram on the next page shows the corps dispositions on 5 April 1916 - nine brigades in the line, holding sectors from Petillon, near Laventie, in the north to Auchy in the south. Six brigades were in reserve.

Surprisingly, brigades in reserve did very little formal training. Days were spent on fatigues or on working parties or what was euphemistically called 'company training' which seldom went beyond platoon and company drills.[29] A few specialists, and those chosen to raid enemy trenches in their next venture into the line, were given an opportunity to practise their skills, but not until the end of May were brigades asked to train larger formations,[30] and by then the coming offensive was only weeks away. Part of the difficulty was that the British army, unlike the French, did not have a local civilian work force and infantry out of the line tended to be used as casual labour. This, and the generally exhausted state of the men after a spell in the front line, left very little time for serious offensive training.

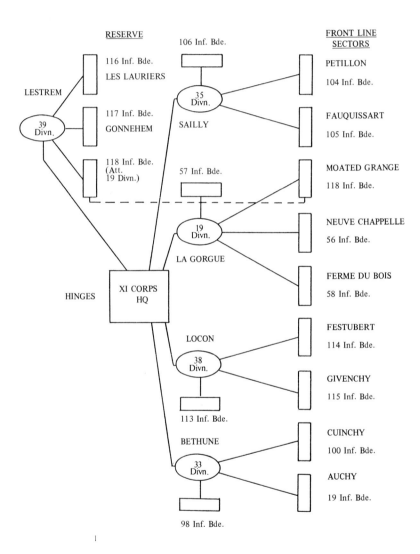

XI Corps dispositions, 5 April 1916

Plans for the Allied offensive in 1916

Ten days after succeeding Sir John French as commander-in-chief in France, Haig attended a conference at the French headquarters at Chantilly. Not much was said about future plans for an offensive but on the following day, 30 December 1915, Joffre wrote to say that he was studying, amongst other possibilities, the launching of a 'powerful offensive' south of the River Somme, and he asked for views on the possibility of British forces joining in with a simultaneous attack on a wide front north of the river. He also pressed for the relief of the French Tenth Army (see Map 1), since its interpolation between the British First and Third Armies would make for difficulties during such an attack.[31] Haig was not anxious to use his divisions both to relieve the French army and to mount an offensive, and he replied saying that although he would arrange to relieve the left of the French Tenth Army he could not offer to do more without further study. On 20 January, however, General Joffre proposed a different arrangement, which was that the British should attack on a large scale north of the Somme as a preliminary to a weighty, and decisive, joint attack at a place and time still to be determined. In a letter sent a few days later, he explained that what he had in mind for the British was a 'wide and powerful offensive...with a minimum of 15 to 18 divisions' during April, followed, possibly, by another in May elsewhere on the British front.[32] Haig would not agree and at a conference at Chantilly on 14 February, Joffre gave way. 'He admitted,' Haig wrote in his diary, 'that attacks to prepare the way for the decisive attack and to attract the enemy's reserves were necessary, but only some 10 to 15 days before the main battle, certainly not in April for a July attack. This seemed quite a victory for me.'[33] At the conference, both Generals agreed that the French and British forces should attack 'side by side' with the French left placed just north of the River Somme.

On 21 February, the Germans pre-empted the Allied plans by attacking the French at Verdun. Haig immediately undertook to relieve the whole of the French Tenth Army, which he did by putting in extra divisions to extend the First Army southwards and the Third Army northwards, until they met near Vimy. A Fourth Army was formed under General Sir Henry Rawlinson on 1 March and this took over the front previously held by the right of the Third Army.

The German attack at Verdun did not weaken Joffre's resolve for a joint offensive; his only doubt was over the best date for launching it. Joffre's attitude was in marked contrast to that of the War Committee in London which still showed a distinct lack of enthusiasm. Prompted by Robertson, Haig submitted his plans to the Committee in early April and asked for authority to proceed. Asquith consented, but with such obvious misgivings that Haig, at a meeting with Kitchener and Robertson some days later, was prompted to ask 'Did H.M.'s Government approve of my combining with the French in a general offensive during the summer?' He did not get a clear answer even then; just an indication that some prominent members of the Cabinet were on his side, but this was enough to enable him to proceed with his plans.[34]

By early May, Joffre was beginning to think again in terms of July for the opening of the offensive, although he realised that this was probably the earliest date on which it could begin. Haig would have preferred a much later date to allow the British army to build up to full strength, but when he mentioned this to the French Commander-in-Chief on 26 May, Joffre reacted violently, as Haig recorded in his diary:

> I said that, before fixing the date, I would like to indicate the state of preparedness of the British army on certain dates and compare its condition. I took 1st and 15th July and 1st and 15th August. The moment I mentioned August 15 Joffre at once got very excited and shouted that 'The French army would cease to exist if we did nothing until then'. The rest of us looked on at this outburst of excitement, and then I pointed out that, in spite of 15th August being the most favourable date for the British army to take action, yet, in view of what he had said regarding the unfortunate condition of the French army, I was prepared to commence operations on the 1st July or thereabouts. This calmed the old man.[35]

Elsewhere, other Allied plans were coming to fruition. On 4th June, the Russians struck with great initial success on a 200 mile front against the Austrians, and the Italians, after regaining the initiative against an Austrian attack which had threatened the Venetian plain, counter-attacked fiercely in mid-June, also with success. As the Germans were wearing themselves out at Verdun and the British and the French were preparing to attack, with great superiority in numbers, on the Somme, it was beginning to look as though the plans laid at a Chantilly conference in December 1915, would be crowned with success. 'Never before, and never again till the fall of 1918,' writes Guinn, 'were the prospects of a military victory over the German army so attractive.'[36]

The 38th Division moves south

Meanwhile, there was an increase in activity all along the British front line. In April, May and early June, the 38th Division carried out at least six raids on German trenches, some successful, some not, depending in the main on how effectively the defensive barbed wire had been cut beforehand. In most places, the opposing lines were too close together for the wire to be cut by shell fire and the favourite alternative device was a 'Bangalore torpedo' - a long tube filled with explosive, which, when it worked (and frequently it did not), blew a wide path through the wire capable of admitting men three abreast. On 10 May, the 10th Welsh placed a torpedo successfully in position under the German wire, but, instead of exploding, it fizzled away in full view of the German line. As the Bangalore torpedo was supposed to be secret, an officer and a lance-corporal had to risk their lives trying to retrieve it. With all element of surprise lost, the raid was called off.[37]

Even when the wire was successfully cut and the German trenches entered, there still remained a hazardous return to the British line amidst retaliatory fire from rifles and machine guns, and it was at this stage that most casualties were suffered. A typical example was the raid by four officers and 51 men of the 15th RWF (London Welsh) on the German trenches north of Farquissart, to where the division had moved in the middle of April. On this raid, which took place on the night of 7/8th May, the wire was cut quietly by hand by an advance party and the raiders, divided into two parties to increase the chances of success, reached the German parapet unobserved:

> Right and left parties filed into action. Both were surprised at the number of enemy in adjacent bays and along the traffic way. The Germans stood sandwiched together, some without equipment and arms, which seems to show that they did not constitute the ordinary garrison of the trench.

Although they could offer no opposition, they blocked the way of the bombers. Realising that there was a delay in front, some bombers on the parapet started to bomb successive bays to right and to left from the ditch, outside the parapet. In this way they helped to clear up the bays in front of the bombers who were in the trenches bombing around the traverses. Right party also encountered a narrow communication trench also congested with Germans. The enemy in this trench was vigorously bombed and his casualties were severe...Left party also found progress slow on account of the density of the enemy. At one point a general rush was made by the occupants of a bay to a bomb store but before they could secure any bombs...they were put out of action by our leading bombers. Numerous attempts to gain this store by the enemy were prevented by steady bombing. Enemy casualties were heavy here.[38]

After 13 minutes of intense activity during which more than 200 bombs were thrown and 50 yards of German trench occupied, the raid commander, Captain Owen, decided to withdraw. Until then, neither raiding party had suffered a single casualty but as they retired, machine guns and rifles opened fire on them and two men were killed and nine wounded; two young officers and one man also failed to return, either killed or captured. Nevertheless, it was estimated that at least 50 Germans had been killed or wounded and the raid was considered a success. When the news reached the corps commander, General Haking was full of praise for the 'fine fighting spirit' of the 15th RWF and he rated the raid as the third most successful on his front since early December. On his recommendation, the battalion was mentioned in Sir Douglas Haig's despatches.[39]

A few days later, General Haking made plans for several raids to be carried out simultaneously in early June. Divisional commanders were asked to make proposals for a 'somewhat larger raid than usual' though each was unaware that other divisions would also be involved. By this means, Haking hoped to keep from the Germans any inkling that something special was afoot. At the last moment, however, he was told by First Army that 'The Commander-in-Chief has decided that, in view of the proximity of offensive operations on our part and the consequent undesirability in these circumstances of disturbing the front and expending a quantity of ammunition which might otherwise be better employed, the simultaneous raids which were to have been carried out on the night of the 3/4 June are not to take place'.[40] The corps commander was, however, allowed to make such raids as he 'considered desirable from time to time,' and acting on this, the 38th Division launched three raids against the German line in quick succession. Two, by the 14th RWF and 14th Welsh Battalions, were successful in reaching and entering the German trenches, but the third, by the 10th Welsh, was held up on the wire, three men being killed and all four officers and nine men wounded. A few nights earlier, however, the 10th Welsh, with a great burst of activity had in one night dug a trench half way across no-man's-land towards the German line. This trench - known thereafter as Rhondda sap - was to be used a month later as a launching point for a heavy attack on the German line, during the ill-fated battle of Fromelles.[41]

This flurry of raids by the 38th (Welsh) Division marked the division's farewell to XI Corps. On 11 and 12 June the two infantry brigades in the line, and the divisional artillery, were relieved by units of the newly arrived 61st Division and the 38th marched south to prepare for the Battle of the Somme. After six months in the trenches, the trek south through the hills of Artois brought a great sense of freedom and, momentarily, of relief from the cares of war:

> The marching in good air was leaving its mark on us all, and we were gaining a release from the humiliating burden of mud that had clogged our pores and turned our thoughts into its own greyness. We walked with a swing, we sang on the march; men began to laugh, to argue and even quarrel, a sure sign of recovery from the torpor of winter. We were going into a battle, true enough, from which few of us could hope to return, but at the moment we were many miles from war, and the hedges were rich with dog-rose and honeysuckle; we were seeing the old flowers in a new country.[42]

On 15 June, the division joined the XVII Corps (Third Army) at St Pol and moved into a new training area just east of the village, where it began to train seriously for offensive action. The training programme which GHQ had issued a few weeks earlier laid down that divisions were to train not only to attack on a large scale against enemy trenches and strong points, but also to follow through once the enemy defences had been broken:

Divisions must, therefore, be practised in the passing of a fresh body of attacking troops through the troops which have carried out the first assault and have reached their objective. The second attack will be carried out on the same principles, the assaulting columns going straight through to the objective in successive lines.[43]

Considerable emphasis was also placed on learning to deal with the unexpected, for Haig was well aware that long periods in the trenches had given junior officers little opportunity to exercise initiative.

On 16 June, the division dug a system of trenches on which to practise its manoeuvres. Here it was at a disadvantage; being in GHQ reserve and not yet destined for any particular part of the front line, the division was unable to reproduce the features of the ground over which it would eventually fight. This was to prove of great significance. When the division later went into battle it was faced with a large, heavily defended wood but woodland fighting, despite the wooded nature of the Somme countryside, had not been included in the training programme.[44]

For the first six days of training, platoons and companies practised going into attack over open ground in extended lines, or 'waves', each successive wave carrying the action forward as the one in front supposed itself in check. This was followed by three days of brigade and divisional manoeuvres in which, for the first time in France, all arms joined: artillery brigades, machine gun companies, signallers and engineers, aided by spotter aircraft from the Royal Flying Corps.

The exercises were carefully planned. Each unit was given a definite objective and detailed orders were issued by divisional and brigade headquarters. Annex A shows the orders issued by the 113rd Infantry Brigade (Brig.Gen. Price-Davies) for a mock attack on trenches representing the German second and third lines on 24 June. For this attack, which was supported by a full artillery brigade, the 113th used all its available forces: two battalions in the initial assault and two for the capture of the final objective. Though the absence of an enemy must have lent an air of unreality to the proceedings, the brigade staff were, nevertheless, given an opportunity to handle large forces in the open and to practise the difficult manoeuvre of passing one battalion through another. As the attack proceeded, unit commanders were deliberately confronted with unexpected difficulties. Some, for example, were told that they had advanced into their own artillery fire; others that formations to right or left had been held up by the enemy and were in need of assistance. Until appropriate action was taken, the unit concerned was deemed to have suffered casualties on a scale determined by watching umpires.[45]

Some valuable lessons were learned during this all-too-short period of training - particularly about the importance of maintaining good communications between infantry and artillery. But the technique of advancing in extended lines, proposed by GHQ and practised diligently at St. Pol, was to prove less than effective on the field of battle.

On 26 June, the men still exhausted from their strenuous activities on the training ground, the division marched west of Doullens, where it came under the command of GOC II Corps, still in GHQ reserve, and then south-eastwards to Toutencourt which it reached on 30 June - the eve of the Battle of the Somme. Here the division waited for orders, prepared to move at six hours notice.[46]

The Battle of the Somme
As we have seen, neither the ground nor the date for the coming battle were of Haig's choosing. He would have much preferred an operation in Flanders which at least offered the possibility of turning the German flank to the sea. There were, however, two drawbacks to such a plan; firstly, the King of Belgium was opposed to offensive action on his soil[47] and, secondly, an attack in this area would, perforce, be on a much narrower front than any combined offensive with the French. The Somme in fact seems to have been chosen by Joffre for this very reason, for it had few other strategic advantages. It is true that Joffre, in advocating this particular part of the front, had drawn attention to the fact that it had been quiet for some time - thus implying that the Germans might not be on the alert[48] - but that was in December, since when the Germans had been busy all along the front improving their defences. By 1 July the defence system north of the Somme presented a very formidable obstacle. Throughout the planning of the Somme battle, Haig kept up his sleeve an alternative plan for an attack at Messines in Belgium should the French effort on the

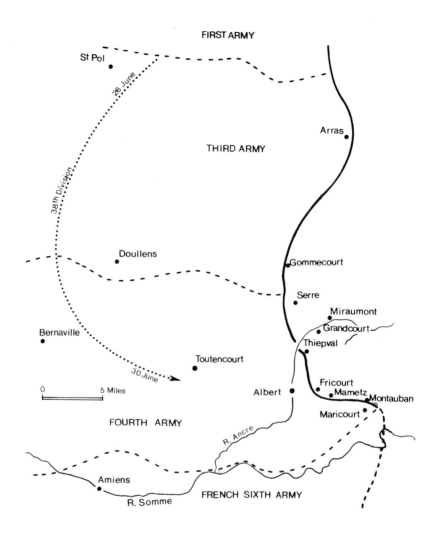

Map 3. The Somme. Route taken by the 38th Division.

Somme dwindle as a result of the heavy fighting at Verdun, but
he had no cause to use it in 1916.

North of the River Somme, the British line ran, as Map 3
shows, westward from Maricourt to Fricourt and then northwards
to Thiepval and Serre, through fertile chalk downs reminiscent
of the hills of southern England, though more open and unfenced.
Around Fricourt and Mametz the hills are steeper and more wooded

than to the north where the ground rises and dips with 'graceful gentleness'. Along this front, General Sir Henry Rawlinson, whose Fourth Army was to make the main assault for the British, had by 1 July assembled five corps: eleven divisions in the line and five in close support. In addition there were two infantry divisions and one cavalry division in army reserve. On his left, the British Third Army was to cooperate by mounting a simultaneous attack by two divisions on Gommecourt. On the British right, the French Sixth Army sat astride the marshy valley of the River Somme with three corps: the XX Corps north of the river; the I Colonial Corps immediately south of the river and the XXXV Corps on the far right. In all, five French divisions would go into the attack along a front of eight to nine miles compared to eleven divisions along fifteen miles on Rawlinson's front. The main burden of the attack would therefore fall on the British.

Haig's plan was to break through the German line between Maricourt and Fricourt and drive northward, rolling up the Germans behind the Fricourt-Thiepval front and creating an ever-widening gap in the German defences as British troops attacking that part of the front joined in.[49] Although Rawlinson was to command all Fourth Army forces during the opening assault, Lt.-Gen. Gough was standing by with a mobile force, drawn from Fourth Army and GHQ reserves, to spearhead the advance once the defences had been breached.

Experience at Neuve Chapelle and Vimy Ridge in 1915 had taught the Germans that a single line of defence, even when reinforced by a network of subsidiary trenches, was not adequate to withstand the increasing strength of British and French artillery. In the summer of that year they began to construct, along the whole length of their front, a second defensive position, as strongly fortified as the first, about two miles behind the front line. Early in 1916, faced with the possibility of a Franco-British offensive on the Western Front they started to build a third line, two miles to the rear again, which was completed in May 1916. The front line trenches themselves were considerably strengthened and the garrison protected from artillery fire by the insertion of thick traverses at frequent intervals to contain the blast from exploding shells. Deep dug-outs were also built, 20 or 30 feet down into the chalk. In front, the barbed wire had been massed into two great belts, each 30 yards deep and 15 yards apart, interlaced with iron stakes and tall trestles to form an impenetrable barrier three to five feet high. In the hilly country of the Somme, the whole system of defence, traversed by interconnecting trenches and provided with an excellent, deep-laid telephone network, rose 'tier upon tier' on the hillsides, to a distance of four to six miles behind the front line.[50]

Because of the strength of the German defences, and the limited range of his own field artillery, Rawlinson, in his early planning, decided not to attempt to carry the second line at the first assault but to limit himself to an advance of about 2,000 yards on a line from Mametz in the south to Serre in the north while maintaining strong defensive positions on either flank. He would then reform, and push forward another thousand yards to capture the German second line between Pozieres and Grandcourt where it came nearest to the front line. During this stage he would again stay on the defensive on both flanks.[51]

This was not good enough for Haig. He was convinced that the Germans would fall back in confusion and wished to take advantage of their disarray to capture not only their front line but also much of their second position, and their heavy artillery, during the first day. He also wanted a big push on both flanks, to capture the high ground around Montauban on the right, and west of Miraumont on the left, which he regarded as particularly important for the development of subsequent stages of the battle.[52]

In spite of Rawlinson's worries about the distance to be covered by the infantry and about the difficulties of cutting the barbed wire in front of the second line, this is substantially the plan finally adopted (see Map 4). The details of the opening attack were worked out at Fourth Army headquarters on 12 June, as was the broad outline of subsequent phases of the battle. Four days later, Haig put in writing his own view of the way the battle should develop after the first day. The attack, he wrote, should be:

> pressed eastward far enough to enable our cavalry to push through into the open country beyond the enemy's prepared lines of defence. Our object will then be to turn northwards, taking the enemy's lines in flank and reverse.[53]

But it was not to be. At 7.30 am on 1 July 1916, after seven days of heavy bombardment which was confidently expected to obliterate the German wire and all defenders in the German trenches, the British infantry rose from its trenches as the guns lifted from the German front line, and, in brilliant sunshine, stumbled heavily loaded across the broken ground of no-man's-land into a hail of machine gun fire. Thousands were mown down near their own trenches; others were held up on the German wire which in many places the guns had failed to breach.

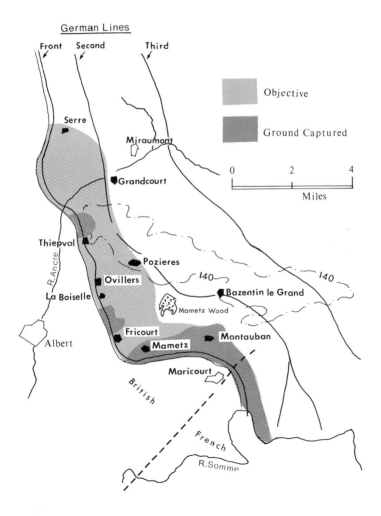

Map 4. Objectives and achievements: 1 July 1916.

Only in the south was there any lasting success, the 18th and 30th Divisions of the XIII Corps (both new army divisions) capturing their objectives around Montauban; and the 7th and 21st Divisions of the XV Corps partly doing so by capturing Mametz village and breaking the German front line west of Fricourt (see Map 4). Elsewhere there was total failure, although the 36th (Ulster) Division of the X Corps broke right through to the German second position near Thiepval only to be beaten back, with very heavy casualties, to the German front line. The British losses on the whole front for that one day were disastrous - nearly 60,000 in all, including more than 20,000 killed or missing - though the figures reaching Rawlinson at Fourth Army headquarters (16,000 by 7.30 pm) failed to reveal the true position.[54]

On the right, the French, with a greater concentration of heavy artillery, did better, the XX Corps quickly overrunning the German front line north of the Somme. South of the river, the French pushed well beyond their first objectives, almost to the German second line.[55]

During the afternoon, Haig visited Fourth Army headquarters and 'expressed the wish that the attack of the Fourth Army should be continued on the 2nd'. The situation, he felt, 'was as yet too obscure for any radical change of plan; the best that could be done for the moment was to keep up the pressure on the enemy, wear out his defence, and, with a view to an attack on his second position, gain possession of those parts of his front position and of the intermediate lines still in his hands'. The village of Fricourt, already enveloped, was to be a prime target.[56] After leaving Fourth Army headquarters, Haig motored to II Corps where he released two divisions - the 38th (Welsh) and the 23rd - from GHQ reserve to Fourth Army, so that Rawlinson could put his existing reserves into the line for 2 July.[57]

At 7 pm, Rawlinson, realising that there was now no hope of an early breakthrough, telephoned Haig to say that he was putting the VIII Corps and X Corps under Gough with effect from 7 am the following morning[58] so that he, Rawlinson, could concentrate his attention on the three corps south of the River Ancre. Gough's independant command eventually became the Fifth Army.

At 10 pm, Rawlinson issued orders for the attack to be continued next day on the left and in the centre of the new Fourth Army frontage south of the Ancre - with the object of capturing La Boiselle, Ovillers, Fricourt and Contalmaison (see

Maps 4 and 5). At Fricourt the Germans offered little resistance
at first and by midday on 2 July the 17th (Northern) Division
had occupied the village and pushed on towards Bottom Wood about
a mile beyond. On its right, the 7th Division advanced from

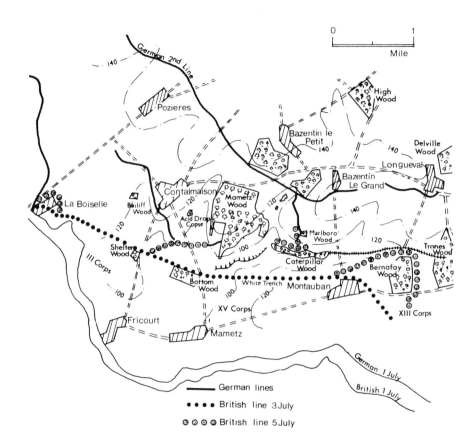

Map 5. The Somme: Positions on the 3rd and 5th July

Mametz village to White Trench, just south of Mametz Wood. At La
Boiselle, however, the 19th (Western Division) had difficulty in
moving forward over shell-torn and congested ground and was not
ready to attack until 4 pm, and then with only one brigade.
Nevertheless, by 9 pm half the village had been captured. At
Ovillers, the 12th (Eastern) Division, having just moved into
the line from reserve, had even greater organisational
difficulties, and the order to capture the village was

cancelled. At the end of the day, Contalmaison remained well out of reach. Throughout this time, Gough's two corps on the left, and the successful XIII Corps on the right, stood on the defensive, the former because Gough considered them to be in no fit state to attack until the morning, the latter because Rawlinson was not prepared to advance further on this front until he had made 'a strong line from Boiselle to Montauban as a basis from which to carry out further attacks'.[59] He was confirmed in this view by aircraft reports that the ridge opposite Montauban was strongly held. Haig, however, had heard that the enemy had 'only a few patrols in Bernafay Wood (north-east of Montauban) and that they were surrendering freely'. He therefore told his chief of staff, Lt.-Gen. Kiggell, to 'urge Rawlinson to greater activity in the direction of Longueval'. He also sent his commander, Royal Artillery, (Maj.-Gen. Birch) to Fourth Army headquarters 'to go into the artillery situation with the same objective'.[60] In Haig's view there was plenty of men, but insufficient ammunition to sustain an attack along the whole Fourth Army front, and he was keen to concentrate on the ridge between Longueval and Bazentin le Grand which would enable him to 'overlook the slopes running thence northwards and to threaten envelopment of [enemy] troops on the Pozieres-Thiepval position'.[61] He believed this would be more successful than a direct attack, from the direction of La Boiselle and Thiepval, on the Pozieres ridge where the defences, as he told Joffre the following day, were 'very much stronger and deeper'.[62] He failed, however, to secure a promise from the French to do anything other than give very limited support to his right wing. This made it difficult for Haig to exploit the success gained at Montauban on 1 July.

Before dawn on 3 July, the 12th (Eastern) Division attacked and entered the German line in front of Ovillers. When the attack moved on to the support trenches, however, the Germans counter-attacked fiercely and the attackers were gradually overwhelmed. A few entered the outskirts of Ovillers but were soon driven back. In this bitter fighting, the 12th Division lost nearly 2,400 officers and men. To the right, the 19th Division increased its grip on La Boiselle and the three divisions of the XV Corps - the 7th, 17th and 21st - strengthened their positions below Mametz Wood, the 17th Division capturing Bottom Wood and the 21st Division, Shelter Wood. On the night of 3/4 July, the 21st Division was taken out of the line to rest and the 38th (Welsh) Division came into XV Corps reserve.

The 38th Division had marched through the night of 1/2 July from Toutencourt to Acheux, about five miles behind the front line at Thiepval. After a day's rest, the division turned south to Treux, four miles south-west of Albert, where it joined XV Corps and billeted in the nearby villages for the night of 4/5 July. On the way, it passed tented encampments of cavalry which had been concentrated just west of Albert. A few days earlier, the cavalry divisions had been given priority on the roads leading to the front, but now they were kicking their heels waiting for a breakthrough that never came. On 5 July the Welsh Division, less artillery, was orded to take over the front from Bottom Wood to Caterpillar Wood from the 7th Division, whose artillery would remain in place. Units of the division moved into the area below Mametz Wood that evening, 'footsore and weary,'[63] to begin the relief, which was completed by 1 am on 6 July. Maj.-Gen. Ivor Philipps sent the following message of encouragement to every man in the division:

You have worked hard for many months with an energy and zeal beyond praise to fit yourself for the task you have voluntarily undertaken. You have undergone the hardships of a winter campaign with fortitude. You have earned the praise of your corps commanders for your courage, discipline and devotion to duty. You have now held for 6 months a section of the British line in France, during which time you have not allowed one of the enemy to enter your trenches except as a prisoner, and on several occasions you have entered the enemy's lines. 11 officers and 44 nco's and men have already received rewards from the King for gallant and distinguished conduct in the field. Your fellow countrymen at home are following your career with interest and admiration. I always believed that a really Welsh Division would be second to none. You have more than justified that belief. I feel that whatever the future may have in store for us I can rely upon you, because you have already given ample proof of your worth. During the short period in the training area you worked hard to qualify yourselves for still further efforts. I thank you most sincerely for the loyal and wholehearted way in which you have all supported me and for the way in which each of you has done his utmost to carry out the task allotted to him. With such a spirit animating all ranks we can one and all look forward with confidence to the future, whatever it may have in store for us. You are today relieving the 7th Division, which has attacked and captured German trenches on a front of a little less than one mile and for a depth of about one and a quarter miles. In this attack the village of Mametz was captured, the enemy have suffered very heavy casualties, 1,500 German officers and men were taken prisoners and six field guns were captured.

The 1st Battalion, Royal Welsh Fusiliers and the 1st Battalion, Welsh Regiment of the 7th Division have both distinguished themselves in this attack, and I am confident that the young battalions of the famous Welsh regiments serving in the 38th (Welsh) Division will maintain the high standard for valour for which all three Welsh regiments have been renowned throughout the war.[64]

Siegfried Sasson, with all the superiority of one who had arrived in France four weeks earlier than the 38th Division, watched some of the incoming units arrive at Bottom Wood:

In the evening we were relieved. The incoming battalion numbered more than double our own strength (we were less than 400) and they were unseasoned new army troops. Our little trench under the trees was inundated by a jostling company of exclamatory Welshmen. Kinjack would have called them a panicky rabble. They were mostly undersized men, and as I watched them arriving at the first stage of their battle experience I had a sense of their victimisation. A little platoon officer was settling his men down with a valient show of self-assurance. For the sake of appearances, orders of some kind had to be given, though in reality there was nothing to do except sit down and hope it wouldn't rain. He spoke sharply to some of them, and I felt that they were like a lot of children. It was going to be a bad look-out for two such bewildered companies, huddled up in the Quadrangle, which had been over-garrisoned by our own comparatively small contingent. Visualising that forlorn crowd of khaki figures under the twilight of the trees, I can believe that I saw then, for the first time, how blindly war destroys its victims. The sun had gone down on my own reckless brandishings, and I understood the doomed condition of these half trained civilians who had been sent up to attack the Wood.[65]

Sassoon might, perhaps, have been less patronising had he been able to read the minds of the incoming troops. They were equally condescending in their views, and not at all overawed at taking over from the 1st Battalion of their own regiment, to which Sassoon belonged:

> Our guides [from the 1st Battalion] lost their way, but having wandered over most of the country we found ourselves in a half dug trench and we were told 'this was the spot'. By now I can forgive the company of the 1st Battalion for the unseemly haste with which it departed. But at the time, coming from an area where reliefs had amounted almost to a ceremonial parade, I was little less than amazed when I found no officers, no instructions, no information or anything else, and found that the tired regulars had departed almost as quickly as the Portuguese used to up north.[66]

After this unpropitious beginning, the Welshmen posted out sentries and spent the night slinging dead over the parapet and deepening the trench. When daylight came, they fired sporadically at the Germans in Mametz Wood while waiting, in unpleasant surroundings, for further orders.

3. Mametz Wood, 5-9 July 1916

Alas said this staff-captain.
Ah dam said this staff-major.
Alas alas said Colonel Talabolion.

On 3 July the Fourth Army began its preparations for the attack on the German second line on Bazentin ridge. On the right, XIII Corps was ordered to occupy Bernafay Wood and Caterpillar Wood as soon as possible and to push patrols forward into Trones Wood (see Map 5). XV Corps in the centre and III Corps on the left were told to prepare for attacks on Mametz Wood and Contalmaison respectively once they had consolidated their positions.[1] Final orders were issued on 5 July for all three corps to advance, on 7 July, to within attacking distance of the second line. XIII Corps was given the task of capturing Trones Wood as far north as the railway line; XV Corps, Mametz Wood and Acid Drop Copse; and III Corps, the cutting north of Contalmaison, Contalmaisom village itself and Bailiff Wood. XV Corps was told to begin its advance through Mametz Wood at once and capture as much of the wood as possible by the morning of the 7th.[2]

Haig attached considerable importance to these preliminaries - more so than Rawlinson. On 4 July, Haig visited Rawlinson at Fourth Army headquarters to impress upon him the 'importance of getting Trones Wood to cover the right flank and Mametz Wood and Contalmaison to cover the left flank of the attack against the Longueval front'.[3] A few days later, when Mametz Wood was proving particularly difficult to capture, Rawlinson wanted to press on with the main attack without it. Haig would not agree and ordered Rawlinson not to attempt to pierce the German line until the wood and Contalmaison were in British hands.[4]

General Kiggell, Haig's chief of staff, also wrote to Rawlinson giving him the Commander-in-Chief's views on the tactical situation:

On the left flank of the Fourth Army main attack Mametz Wood is of great tactical importance. Unless it is in our possession the left flank of the main attack would be very insecure. Moreover, this flank could not extend to the west of a line from Marlboro' Wood to Bazentin le Grand and the front would be seriously restricted. Furthermore, with Mametz Wood in our possession Bazentin le Petit Wood and the enemy trenches to the south of it will be seriously threatened by us, and it may prove possible to assault them. Even the threat on them and on Bazentin le Petit Wood from the west, will be of great support and encouragement to the left flank of the main attack. For these reasons it is considered that only such a state of demoralisation on the enemy's side as would justify great risks being taken to profit by it immediately would justify the launching of the main attack before Mametz Wood had been captured.[5]

Rawlinson was not wholly convinced. 'I received this morning Kig's appreciation of the situation with which I entirely agree,' he wrote in his journal on 9 July. 'He has put in irreproachable language what I said to DH yesterday. The only point I am doubtful about is whether we are wise to wait for the capture of Mametz Wood before launching our attack against Longueval.'[6]

These differing views about the importance of Mametz Wood stemmed directly from a lack of understanding between Haig and Rawlinson over plans for the main assault upon Bazentin ridge. Originally, both had envisaged a frontal attack between the Bazentins and Longueval and both had acknowledged the importance of Mametz Wood on the left flank. As time went by, however, Haig became attracted to the idea of an attack, from Mametz Wood itself, on the German line between Contalmaison Villa (a building northeast of Contalmaison village) and Bazentin le Petit Wood and then eastward behind the German line towards Longueval, the German defences being enfiladed by artillery fire from the northern edge of Mametz Wood.[7] Map 6 shows clearly the uninterrupted view of the German line from the northern edge of Mametz Wood which would have given the British artillery considerable advantage over their German counterparts. It also shows that an attack from this point would have been over relatively flat ground to Bazentin le Grand and beyond.

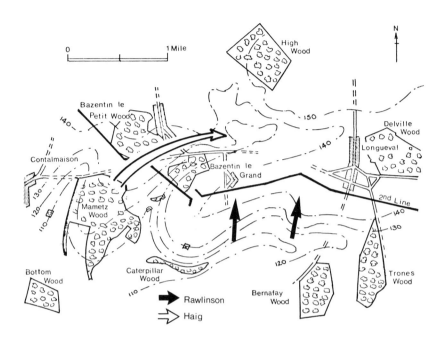

Map 6. Alternative plans for the capture of Bazentin ridge.

Because his plan would have used Mametz Wood as a springboard for attack, Haig's attention was naturally sharply focussed on its capture.

Rawlinson on the other hand stuck to the idea of a frontal attack on the line between Bazentin le Grand Wood and Longueval, but with an important change of timing: the divisions concerned would form up on the open ground at night, under cover of darkness, and the attack would be made at first light. This night assembly, of course, considerably reduced the threat to the left flank of a German attack from Mametz Wood and, although Rawlinson was prepared to support his main attack with a minor thrust from the wood if it was in his hands in time, he was equally prepared to take the risk of pressing on without it. To Rawlinson, therefore, the significance of Mametz Wood diminished as the days wore on. His main concern was to waste as little time as possible before mounting the main attack on the German second line.

Not until 10 July - three days after the projected date for the capture of Mametz Wood - did Haig learn of Rawlinson's daring plan. He was not very happy; partly because it involved an uphill attack over 1,000 yards of ground (see the contours in Map 6) but mainly because he just did not believe it would be possible to form up divisions 'in mass in the dark; which we cannot do in time of peace'.[8] But Rawlinson continued to argue the merits of his plan, strongly supported by General Montgomery, his chief of staff, and by Lt.-Gen. Horne, commander of the XV Corps. On 12 July Haig finally acquiesced, insisting only that strong points should be built to protect the troops assembling on the southern slopes. While these discussions were taking place, the 17th and 38th Divisions were hurling themselves at Mametz Wood in a desperate attempt to secure its early capture. Ironically, by the time Haig had come around to Rawlinson's way of thinking, the wood was in British hands. It is a sad commentary on the conduct of the war that both commanders could issue orders for preliminary attacks, which were to cost thousands of lives, without first having an agreed plan for the main battle.

All this was in the future, however, as the 38th (Welsh) Division moved into the line from Bottom Wood to Caterpillar Wood on 5 July. The aim of the Fourth Army was then quite clear: capture Trones Wood on the right and Mametz Wood on the left - and do it quickly. On 6 July, Rawlinson wrote in his journal:

> The attacks by III Corps and XV Corps against Contalmaison and Mametz Wood will be carried out as arranged. They have fresh divisions and I hope all will go well...

Thus was the 38th (Welsh) Division committed to battle.

Mametz Wood

North of the road from Mametz village to Montauban, the ground falls away, gently at first and then more steeply, until it reaches Willow Stream (see Map 7). The final descent is down a steep chalk bank, or 'cliff', varying from about thirty to fifty feet in height.

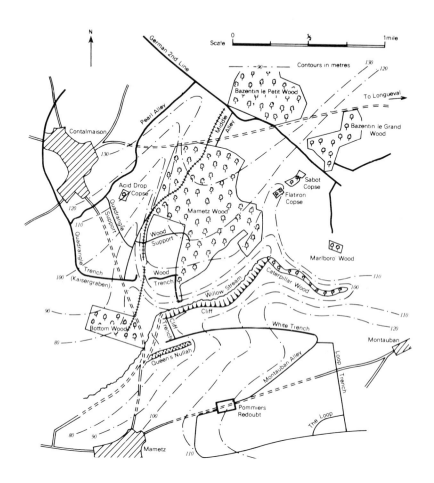

Map 7. Mametz Wood and defences.

From Willow Stream the ground rises for more than a mile northward to the ridge which runs from Pozieres, through the Bazentins, to Longueval on which lay the deeply fortified trenches of the German second line. Mametz Wood 'a menacing wall of gloom',[9] lay on a slight spur on the far side of the valley, flanked by two small re-entrants rising up towards the ridge. Because of these undulations an attack on the wood, whether from the south, the east or the west, would involve the movement of troops down the slope of a valley and then up rising ground on the far side, exposed all the while to rifle and machine gun fire from the wood and the nearby copses.

The wood itself was (and still is) very large and overgrown. From north to south it measured about a mile long, the northern face being about 300 yards from the German second line (from which it could quickly be reinforced), the southern extremity dipping down almost to Willow Stream. East to west, it measured about three quarters of a mile at its widest point, although a large open space at the southwest corner considerably reduced the width of the southernmost portion. The total area of woodland was about 220 acres.[10]

On the night of 3/4 July a small patrol from the 2nd Battalion, Royal Irish Regiment (7th Division) entered the wood and reconnoitred the southern areas. The patrol reported that the wood was dense with undergrowth which would make it difficult for infantry to move. It found Strip Trench (see Map 8) strongly wired and well traversed.[11] The wood itself was a mixture of oak about nine feet in girth, with some beech and ash. The average height was estimated to be between thirty and forty five feet.[12] The wood, which had been untended for at least two years, was traversed by a central ride running from north to south, and two cross rides more or less at right angles to the first. These were clearly marked on the operational maps used by the XV Corps but they were suffering from neglect and were less easily discernable on the ground.

To the west of Mametz Wood the keystone of the German defences was a well-constructed trench known as the Kaisergraben which ran south of Contalmaison towards the western face of Mametz Wood. Behind it lay a network of subsidiary trenches protecting the whole of the southwestern flank of the wood (see Map 7). Some of these were connected to the wood and, so long as this remained in German hands, the trenches could be readily reinforced or evacuated as the situation demanded. The Kaisergraben itself had been constructed well before the opening of the Battle of the Somme and was provided with good dug-outs cut twenty feet down into the chalk.[13] Not surprisingly, it proved difficult to capture but on the night of 4/5 July the 17th Division, in cooperation with the 7th Division which

attacked Wood Trench, captured the portion of it between Pearl
Alley and Wood Trench, and renamed it Quadrangle Trench. Wood
Trench itself - the site of Siegfried Sassoon's 'reckless
brandishes' - remained in German hands.

There was no similar defensive network to the east of Mametz
Wood; nor was one necessary. At this point, the German second
line sloped down the face of the ridge and from this position,
and from Sabot and Flatiron copses, German machine guns could
easily command the eastern approaches to the wood.

5-6 July

On the night of 5/6 July the XV Corps had two divisions in the
line: on the left, the 17th (Northern) Division (Maj.-Gen.
Pilcher), which had already been heavily engaged in the
fighting, held Quadrangle Trench up to its junction with
Quadrangle Alley; on the right the 38th Division (113th and
115th Brigades) held Bottom Wood, Cliff Trench and most of White
Trench. Both divisions were backed by artillery from the
divisions which had been in the line before them; the 21st
Divisional artillery covering the 17th Division on the left and
the 7th Divisional artillery covering the 38th Division on the
right. At that time, the boundary between XV Corps and XIII
Corps lay on the western edge of Caterpillar Wood which was
occupied by the 18th Division (XIII Corps).

On 6 July, in preparation for the next day's attack by XV
Corps, there was a general reshuffle to the right, the 17th
(Northern) Division taking over Bottom Wood, and the 38th
(Welsh) Division the western half of Caterpillar Wood and also
Marlborough Wood (the most forward position of all). Facing them
were units of the German 3rd Guards Division and the 28th
Reserve Division.[14] Mametz Wood itself was held by a
battalion of the Lehr Regiment of the Prussian Guard, another
battalion of the regiment being in position around Flatiron
Copse.[15] On their right the 163rd Regiment (attached to
28th Reserve Division) defended Contalmaison and the open ground
between Quadrangle Trench and the western edge of the wood.

For the 7th July, XV Corps planned a two-pronged attack upon
the wood at 8 am, the 17th Division attacking Acid Drop Copse
and the strip of wood LMNK from the west (the lettering is that
used on the operational maps of the time - see Map 8), and the
38th Division attacking the 'Hammerhead' (so called because of

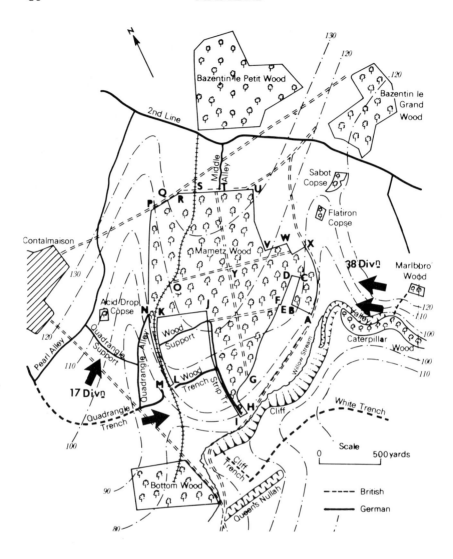

Map 8. Attack on Mametz Wood, 7th July.

its shape - AXCB in Map 8) on the eastern side of the wood. Once they had entered the wood, both divisions were to advance towards the central ride before swinging northward up through the wood.The 38th Division was given the additional task of sweeping across the southern portion of the wood to take Strip Trench from the rear. As a preliminary to the main attack, and to protect the left flank, the 17th Division was to attack and capture Quadrangle Support trench and those parts of Pearl Alley and Quadrangle Alley leading up to it. This was to be done under cover of darkness, starting at 2 am after an intense artillery bombardment of the enemy positions. It was assumed that this attack, completely unsupported on either flank and against strongly defended positions, would be successful, if not at first, at least as the night wore on. The only concession to failure was that the main attack would be postponed from 8 am to 8.30 am if at that time Quadrangle support trench was still in enemy hands. This contingency plan was called 'Scheme B'.[16]

The main attack was to be preceded by a heavy bombardment of the German second line, and of strong points in and around the wood, to a rigorous timetable laid down by the artillery commander of XV Corps.[17] This bombardment was to start at 7.20 am and last for forty minutes. Both supporting divisional artilleries (the 21st on the left now reinforced by one artillery brigade from 38th Division; the 7th on the right) were to 'search' the wood thoroughly during this time using every available 4.5 howitzer and 18-pounder, with concentrated fire on those edges of the wood which were to come under attack from the infantry. In this preliminary bombardment special attention was to be paid to Acid Drop Copse on the left and Flatiron and Sabot Copses on the right which were known to harbour German machine guns. The corps heavy artillery would back up by bombarding the same targets, and their massive 9.2 inch batteries would fire on the German second line. Once the attack had been launched, all guns would be lifted by strict timetable ahead of the planned position of the infantry, until by 9.30 all fire would be concentrated on targets beyond the wood. In the event of 'Scheme B' being put into operation, the artillery would concentrate at 8 am on the area around Quadrangle Support before moving on, half an hour later, to the main programme.

On the 38th Division's front, the task of attacking the wood fell to Brig.-Gen. Horatio Evans and his 115th Brigade. At 8 am on 6 July - some two hours before XV Corps issued its detailed orders - the GSO 1 of the 38th Division (Lt.Col. ap Rhys Pryce) arrived at brigade headquarters and gave Evans a brief outline of the task he was to perform, namely to attack the southeast portion of the wood from Caterpillar Wood at 8 am the following morning. No mention was made of an advance to the central ride or of the subsequent drive northward through the wood. This suggests that the divisional staff were not at this time aware of the extent of the XV Corps' plans.

.   Together, Evans and Rhys Pryce went over to Caterpillar Wood to reconnoitre the ground. On the way, they were told by a neighbouring brigade that nothing definite was known about the number of German troops in Mametz Wood but that it appeared to be held right up to the edges, though not in any great strength. When they reached Caterpillar Wood, the brigadier reconnoitred the ground immediately to the north and west of the wood, while the staff officer went on to Marlborough Wood. During his survey, Evans observed that troops could be assembled safely in a dip in the ground north of Caterpillar Wood provided they were not pushed too far up the hill towards Bazentin le Grand Wood. It also became clear to him that as the subsequent attack would have to be made over ground which could easily be swept by machine gun fire from the north, it would be prudent to keep as close as possible to the valley running along the northern edge of Caterpillar Wood (see Map 8), and to attack on a narrow frontage, one battalion wide, supported by machine guns and trench mortars in Caterpillar and Marlborough woods. When he met up with Lt.Col. ap Rhys Pryce later, Brig.-Gen. Evans explained his plans and pointed out where he would form up his four battalions in the valley before the attack. He asked the staff officer to make 'special provision' for his right flank to protect it from machine gun fire.[18] The two men then parted, Rhys Pryce returning to prepare divisional orders, Evans to arrange the disposition of his battalions. He reached his headquarters between 2 and 3 o'clock in the afternoon and immediately ordered his machine gun and trench mortar commanders to make their own reconnaissance and report back. He alerted the commanding officers of the 16th Welsh (Cardiff City) Battalion, which he intended should lead the attack, and the 11th SWB (2nd Gwent) and 10th SWB (1st Gwent), which were to be in support, telling them also to survey the land and then stand by for further orders. The commanding officer of the 16th Welsh, realising that the right flank of his battalion would be exposed to fire from Flatiron Copse, asked to be allowed to assemble in the dark and attack at first light. He had to be told that plans were synchronised with those of the 17th Division and that it was too late to change.[19]

Later that afternoon, Maj.-Gen. Philipps visited brigade headquarters briefly and hinted at the possibility of a more ambitious objective than the Hammerhead at the edge of the wood. Pressed for details, he said that they would all appear in divisional orders which would be issued shortly.[20] Soon after he had gone, brigade received a message to move the 16th Welsh and 11th SWB into their preliminary positions near Loop Trench (Map 7) by 9 pm and then on to Caterpillar Wood by 2 am on 7 July. Brig.-Gen. Evans went off to supervise their assembly leaving draft orders with the brigade major who was instructed to issue them, with any necessary corrections, as soon as divisional orders had been received.

The divisional orders were issued at 8.30 pm. The assembly points for the four battalions were roughly as discussed earlier by Evans and Rhys Pryce, that is, two battalions in Caterpillar Wood valley, another in Caterpillar Wood itself, and the fourth in reserve a little further back towards Montauban Alley and Loop Trench,[21] but on hearing of these dispositions corps headquarters immediately intervened:

> The corps commander considers that it is dangerous to collect more than two battalions in the western end of Caterpillar Wood and valleys in the vicinity owing to the danger of hostile shell fire if the troops are overcrowded. Two battalions are sufficient for the attack on the eastern projection of the wood with a third in support in Montauban Alley and a fourth further back. Any further reinforcements required in the wood should enter by the southern tongue [H in Map 8] which the division should be able to capture without difficulty when the troops have entered the wood from the east, and assisted by those from the west, are clearing up the southern portion of the wood.[22]

Divisional orders were amended accordingly. Evans arrived back at his headquarters at 11 pm to find his brigade major struggling to reconcile the draft brigade orders with those from the division. He was appalled when he saw the detail and complexity of the divisional orders. Capt. Wyn Griffith, on the brigade staff, witnessed his reaction:

The general was cursing...at his orders. He said that only a
madman could have issued them. He called the divisional
staff a lot of plumbers, herring-gutted at that. He argued
at the time, and asked for some control over the artillery
that is going to cover us, but he got nothing out of
them.[23]

This is perhaps a little hard on the divisional staff whose
orders merely repeated, with some elaboration, those given
earlier in the day by corps headquarters. The rigid artillery
programme was none of their doing and some of the elaboration -
for a smoke screen to be laid south of Flatiron and Sabot
copses, for example - was distinctly helpful and in accordance
with Evans's own request. However it was not just the artillery
programme that worried Evans. He was aghast at what he took to
be instructions to attack on a two battalion frontage when he
had been at such pains to explain to Rhys Pryce his reasons for
wanting only one battalion in the front line. 'It appears to me
now,' he was to write later, 'that the dispositions were all cut
and dried by divisional headquarters and that the reconnaissance
was simply made to satisfy them and that I was a mere
figurehead. I was given no discretion in the matter. These
dispositions were the first intimation that the attack was to be
made on a two battalion frontage.'[24] There is, in fact, no
evidence that this is what divisional headquarters intended. A
close examination of the orders issued on 6 July shows no
reference at all to the position of the battalions at the moment
of attack, only to their dispositions beforehand in and around
Caterpillar Wood.[25]
    Be that as it may, Evans faced the formidable task of
implementing, within a few short hours, a plan far more
ambitious and much more detailed than anything he had been led
to expect and which, as he saw it, required a complete revision
of all his previous plans. He worked as quickly as possible to
produce new orders but it was 2 am (on 7 July) before they were
issued. Under the revised arrangements, 11th South Wales
Borderers were to be on the left of the attack (with their left
flank as close as possible to Caterpillar Wood) and 16th Welsh
on the right, each facing northwest and each covering about 250
yards of frontage. As the right of the 16th Welsh would now be

perilously close to the German-held Flatiron Copse, they were to form up under cover of the smoke barrage arranged for 7.45 am.[26]

As soon as these order had been issued, Evans left to rearrange the position of his troops.

7 July

Early on the morning of the 7th, the 17th (Northern) Division, to the west of the wood, launched its planned attack on Quadrangle Support. Two battalions of the 52nd Brigade had been chosen for this attack, the 50th Brigade being held in reserve for the 8 am assault on the west face of Mametz Wood. It had rained during the previous afternoon, and again during the night,[27] and the clinging mud made movement difficult. As the two battalions moved out of their trenches at 2 am, flares lit up the darkness and the advancing troops came under machine gun fire from Quadrangle support, which was held in great force by the Germans, who were themselves preparing to counter attack at about the same time. Hampered by their own shells, which were falling short, the leading waves managed to reach the German barbed wire only to find it still intact, despite a heavy artillery bombardment. They fell back and eventually withdrew. At 4 am, the Germans counter attacked the British left flank but were repulsed. Heavy fighting continued for some hours and 'greatly interfered with preparations for the main attack'.[28]

At 5.25 am, the 17th Division received further orders from corps announcing that Scheme B was to be put into operation and that another attack on Quadrangle Support should take place as arranged at 8 am. The two remaining battalions of the 52nd Brigade were brought into action but in broad daylight and across open ground they had little chance of succeeding where a night attack had failed. Heavy fire from machine guns perched above them in Mametz Wood cut them down as they moved into the attack and casualties were very high. Again, the attackers withdrew.

Meanwhile, just before 7 am Brig.-Gen. Evans, who had been out all night organising his troops in Caterpillar Wood, went up to his new temporary headquarters at Pommiers Redoubt on the Mametz-Montauban road. From here there was a good view of Mametz Wood about a mile away, although the valleys around Caterpillar Wood, where his battalions were forming up, were obscured by the immediate foreground:

> We had reached the high ground at Pommiers Redoubt, and,
> standing in a trench, scanning the wood with our glasses, it
> seemed as thick as virgin forest. There was no sign of life
> in it, no one could see whether it concealed ten thousand
> men or ten machine guns. Its edges were clean cut, as far as
> the eye could see, and the ground between us and the wood
> was bare of any cover. Our men were assembled in trenches
> above a dip in the ground, and from these they were to
> advance, descend into the hollow, and cross the bare slope
> in the teeth of the machine gunners in the wood. On their
> right, as they advanced across the bullet-swept zone, they
> would be exposed to enfilade fire, for the direction of
> their advance was nearly parallel to the German trenches
> towards Bazentin, and it would be folly to suppose that the
> German machine guns were not sited to sweep that slope
> leading to the wood.[29]

Soon after he arrived, Evans received news that the attack was
retimed for 8.30 am under Scheme B and sent this information on
to the battalions. He was also asked to get in touch with the
officer appointed by corps headquarters to arrange the smoke
barrage, but as brigade headquarters new nothing of the officer,
or of the whereabouts of his unit, they failed to locate
him.[30]

At 8 o'clock, Capt. Griffith watched the artillery begin its
bombardment of the edge of the wood:

> A thousand yards away from where I stood, our two battalions
> were waiting. I read the orders again. The attack was to be
> carried out in three stages, beginning at half-past eight,
> reaching in succession three positions inside the wood,
> under the protection of an artillery barrage. Smoke screens
> were to be formed here and there. Everything sounded so
> simple and easy.
>
> A few minutes after eight, all our telephone wires to the
> battalions were cut by the enemy's reply to our fire. There
> was no smoke screen, for some reason never explained -
> perhaps someone forgot about it. This was the first
> departure from the simplicity of the printed word. Messages

came through, a steady trickle of runners bringing evil news; our fire had not masked the German machine guns in Mametz Wood, nor in the wood near Bazentin. The elaborate timetable suddenly became a thing of no meaning, as unrelated to our conditions as one of Napolean's orders...[31]

The attack had in fact been launched at 8.30 am as planned, but it was 9.20 before even this simple piece of news reached brigade headquarters. As soon as the barrage lifted, the leading waves of the 16th Welsh and the 11th SWB battalions moved over the hill and down the slope towards Mametz Wood. Immediately, they came under withering fire from the wood and from Flatiron and Sabot copses. About 200-300 yards from the wood, the attack petered out and the leading troops took what cover they could in a line of shell holes. The successive waves in turn came under heavy fire and were withdrawn back over the crest and into comparative safety.[32]

Private William Joshua, who was in a Lewis machine gun team in the 16th Welsh, was in one of the leading waves:

Number 4 platoon, A company, led the attack, our Lewis gun was on the left flank to prevent them being cut off.

We advanced about 50 yards when the German machine guns opened up. Sergeant Harries shouted out they are yards high and it appeared so, then going down a gentle slope to the wood the enemy got range with deadly effect.

One of my gun team gave me the signal to take a casualty's place in the team, and as I struggled on, I felt a severe shock in my thigh and I was down looking for my leg, thinking I had lost it. Another platoon came along and rested for a breather leaving about ten casualties behind including a sergeant from the cycle company of which a number had joined us to bring us up to strength. Each wave passing me left its quota of dead behind.

Our company runner came along and asked me where Capt. Herdman was, as the order was to retire. I replied that he was somewhere ahead. A large number of our planes were flying low.

Now the German and our own artillery started up, and to add to the horror rain started to fall heavily making the churned up ground into clinging mud. I dumped my equipment and started to crawl back, hugging the ground. Some stretcher bearers found me and took me to a large shell hole. They were members of the Tylorstown Silver Band who had enlisted en bloc in our early recruiting days...My two sergeants, Harries and Thomas were killed also my closest pals G Leyshon and Reg Davies. Two brothers Tregaskis died. They were always first on parade when we formed in Porthcawl; made corporals the same day; officers the same day and died together.[33]

Brigade headquarters, desperate for news, had despatched the Staff Captain (Capt. H V Hinton) to Caterpillar Wood at 8.45 am. His first report, written at about 9.30 am, was received forty minutes later. He confirmed that troops were digging in about 300 yards from the wood and suggested another artillery bombardment. This was immediately relayed to the artillery group commander. Brig.-Gen. Evans also instructed his machine gun company to push more guns towards Caterpillar Wood in an attempt to stifle the deadly fire from the north. By 9.50 am, however, things were getting worse. The Germans had intensified their own machine gun activities and were opening up with artillery on the troops out in the open. Casualties were mounting steadily and the 10th South Wales Borderers were ordered up to reinforce the two leading battalions.[34] Their progress across the maze of trenches was considerably hampered by heavy mud and it was well into the afternoon before they arrived in the battle area.[35]

Meanwhile, both XV Corps and 38th Division headquarters were preparing for another artillery bombardment. At 10.20 am, corps informed Maj.-Gen. Philipps that the heavy artillery would bombard the eastern portion of Mametz Wood from 10.45 to 11.15 am and added, oblivious to the earlier mix-up, that if the division 'wanted more smoke barrage they could employ the special party which was with them'. The division was also told to support the attack by fire from the divisional artilleries which had the advantage of direct observation, which the heavy artillery did not.[36] The news of a fresh bombardment was quickly passed to brigade headquarters and thence to the battalions but there was no chance of it reaching them in time:

We were a thousand yards away from the battalions, with no

telephone communication; there were maps at divisional headquarters, they knew where we were, they knew where the battalions were, and they knew that our lines were out. A simple sum in arithmetic...our operation was isolated; no one was attacking on either flank of our brigade, so that there was complete freedom of choice as to time. With all the hours of the clock to choose from, some master mind must needs select the only hour to be avoided.[37]

Fortunately, by 11 am the telephone wires had been repaired and the commanding officer of the 16th Welsh (Lt.Col. Smith) was able to report that although British shells were falling on his troops he was nevertheless advancing slowly. The artillery bombardment again failed to knock out the machine guns and mounting casualties soon brought the attack to a halt. In the afternoon, the fresh troops of the 10th South Wales Borderers for a time brought new vigour to the offensive but their commanding officer, Lt.Col. Wilkinson, was killed bringing the men forward and once more the advance faded away.

On instructions from XV Corps, divisional headquarters ordered brigade to make a third attack at 5 pm, insisting that this time troops must go into the wood, the eastern edge of which would be heavily bombarded for 30 minutes beforehand.[38] These orders did not reach brigade headquarters until 4 pm and, as the telephone wires had again been cut, Brig.-Gen. Evans decided to go down to Caterpillar Wood himself to reorganise the attack and push in the last battalion: the 17th Royal Welsh Fusiliers. He took Capt. Griffith with him:

The heavy guns of the preceding days had turned the chalky soil into a stiff glue. The hurry in our minds accentuated the slowness of our progress, and I felt as if some physical force was dragging me back. Haste meant a fall into a shell hole, for we had abandoned the attempt to move along the trench. Shrapnel was bursting overhead, and a patter of machine gun bullets spat through the air. We passed through Caterpillar Wood...Along the bare ridge rising up to Mametz Wood our men were burrowing into the ground with their entrenching tools, seeking whatever cover they might make. A few shells were falling, surprisingly few. Wounded men were crawling back from the ridge, men were crawling forward with ammunition. No attack could succeed over such ground as this, swept from front and side by machine guns at short range.[39]

By now it was 4.40 pm, and the battalions were very disorganised; casualties among the officers had been high and men were exhausted and seemed, to Evans, to be somewhat shaken. He called the commanding officers together and ordered them to prepare for an attack on the wood, at whatever cost, with the two freshest battalions (10th SWB and 17th RWF) in the front line. By the time the battalions had reorganised, however, the effect of the artillery bombardment had worn off, and machine guns and trench mortars were still not disposed to Evans's satisfaction. He could see that defences on the edge of Mametz Wood were still intact and that the artillery had fired too deeply into the wood. Realising that a coordinated effort by infantry and artillery would take time to organise, and that success without it was unlikely, he decided to postpone his attack until the evening, or possibly the following morning.[40] Borrowing a field telephone connected to the heavy artillery at Pommiers Redoubt, he urged this course of action on 38th Division headquarters. Division consulted corps. At 6.40 pm, XV Corps headquarters telephoned to 38th Division telling them 'to withdraw and reorganise the battalions engaged at the south east corner of Mametz Wood and to make adequate arrangements for holding the line during the night'.[41] The 17th RWF was detailed to hold the original line on Caterpillar Wood, and the three tired battalions, which between them had suffered more than 400 casualties, returned to their bivouacs during the early hours of the following morning.

On the way back to Pommiers Redoubt, Brig.-Gen. Evans, thoroughly exhausted by 36 hours of continuous and strenuous activity, unburdened himself to Capt. Griffith:

I spoke my mind about the whole business...you heard me. They wanted us to press on at all costs, talked about determination, and suggested that I didn't realise the importance of the operation. As good as told me that I was tired 'and didn't want to tackle the job. Difficult to judge on the spot, they said! As if the whole trouble hadn't arisen because someone found it so easy to judge when he was six miles away and had never seen the country, and couldn't read a map. You mark my words, they'll send me home for this: they want butchers not brigadiers. They'll remember now that I told them, before we began, that the attack could not succeed unless the machine guns were masked. I shall be in England in a month.

Six weeks later he went home,[42] but there is no evidence that he was relieved of his command for outspokenness or for any obvious want of determination, for these faults, when perceived, were usually rewarded with instant dismissal, as happened to Brigadiers Oxley and Fell of the neighbouring 23rd and 17th Divisions. There was no shortage of replacements, and no qualms about changing a commander at the height of battle:

I was with many others a 'vulture' waiting in Amiens to get a brigade [wrote Brig.-Gen. Trotter after the war]. My turn came on 6 July to take over command of 51st Brigade...I do think, looking back, it is rather hard on a brigade to be taken over by a complete stranger in the middle of very confused fighting. I know I felt for Fell, my predecessor in command, when I arrived at his BHQ, and he was unaware that he was superseded by me, and of which I had to inform him.[43]

When Evans left the 115th Brigade in August 1916 he was 56 years old and the brigade was in a quiet sector of the front, well away from the Somme. He had taken the brigade through its first battle, and this would have been a natural time for giving the command to a younger man.

On the west side of the wood, the 17th Division had fared no better. Although both preliminary assaults by the 52nd Brigade on Quadrangle Support failed to make secure the left flank, the 50th Brigade, as planned, went into action at 8.30 am. One battalion (7th East Yorks) struck at the junction of Quadrangle Alley and Quadrangle Support trenches (see Map 8) and almost succeeded in capturing it, but was driven back by bombs and enfilade machine gun fire from Mametz Wood and from the north. It succeeded however in holding on to a point just 50 yards short of the junction. Another battalion (8th Dorset), was held ready to advance on Wood Trench, Wood Support and the western edge of Mametz Wood, once the situation around Quadrangle Support had been resolved. As little progress had been made by mid-afternoon, the 51st Brigade, now under its new commander, was brought up from reserve to replace the 52nd Brigade, which had suffered heavy losses.[44]

As with the 38th Division, XV Corps ordered another attack for 5 pm after a 30 minute bombardment. The divisional commander, uncertain whether or not Quadrangle Support was in his hands, argued for a postponement and XV Corps reluctantly agreed to give him until 6.30 pm to sort things out.[45] Eventually the 17th Division was ordered to attack, at 8 pm, both Quadrangle Support and the strip of wood at LMNK (Map 8). III Corps on its left, which had earlier captured, and then lost Contalmaison, was to . make a simultaneous attack upon the village. In the words of the official historian: 'The Dorset and E. Yorkshire went forward, the 10th Sherwood Foresters, of the 51st Brigade, attacking on the left at the same time. As they struggled through the mud the leading lines of all three battalions were smitten by machine gun fire from the front and from both flanks and were caught by a hostile artillery barrage. There was no hope of success so the operation was abandoned.'[46] The III Corps failed to get itself ready in time for its attack on Contalmaison and this too was cancelled.[47]

So by the end of the day, both III and XV Corps were back where they had been at the beginning.

It is not difficult to find reasons for the failures on 7 July. The plan itself was ill-conceived, fragmented and badly coordinated. On both sides of Mametz Wood, the attacking troops were exposed to enfilade fire at short range. Indeed, it would be difficult to imagine a more suicidal direction of attack than that chosen by XV Corps for the 115th Brigade: parallel to, and not far away from, the German line. If the artillery had silenced the German machine guns there might perhaps have been some hope of success, but this was far beyond the capacity of the artillery in 1916. 'It is beyond dispute that on several occasions where the field artillery has made a considerable 'lift' that is to say, has outstripped the infantry advance, the enemy has been able to man his parapets with rifle and machine gun,' Kiggell wrote from GHQ a few days later. XV Corps put it more bluntly:

The problem of dealing with hostile machine guns is still unsolved. Divisions will report at once any useful experience that has been gained, for the benefit of others.[48]

But the operations were also badly affected by poor communications; telephone lines were cut on both sides of the wood, with disastrous results for the 115th Brigade. With three-quarters of an hour's lag between the brigade and its battalions, messages coming down from corps to division, to brigade, to battalion, crossed with messages on the way up, to the general confusion of all. On this side of the wood it is arguable that too many levels of command were involved. Divisional headquarters, with only one brigade in action, was sandwiched ineffectively between XV Corps and the 115th Brigade, contributing little but adding to the general delay. Indeed, it might have been better if XV Corps, once it had realised that coordination between 17th Division and 38th Division was more or less impossible ('38th Division...when last heard of were about 200 yards from the wood,' XV Corps signalled to 17th Division lamely at one point)[49] had left the conduct of the battle in the hands of brigade commanders. This would at least have allowed Brig.-Gen. Evans to shorten his own lines of communication by moving down to Caterpillar Wood before he did, though whether he would have been able to achieve anything without direct control over the artillery (which he wanted) is questionable, and there was little chance of XV Corps giving him that. The view of the artillery high command was that 'the full destructive power of the available artillery must not be sacrificed to, nor be impeded by, the whims of subordinate commanders'.[50]

The lack of smoke - again due to faulty or inadequate communication between corps and brigade - also contributed to the failure of the 115th Brigade attack. The battalions had been ordered before the attack to form up 'as soon as the smoke barrage on the eastern edge of Mametz Wood and around Flatiron Copse and Sabot Copse is formed' (Brigade Order No 62). It is likely that the failure of the smoke barrier to materialise upset the composure of inexperienced battalion commanders, with the result that the all important first attack lacked sting. But probably the biggest factor of all was the haste with which the plans, such as they were, had to be carried out. 'It was a deliberate attack which required careful preparation and personal reconnaissance of the whole area by me with my COs,' Evans wrote afterwards. 'This it was physically impossible to do' (ie in the time available). He added that the position chosen for brigade headquarters, which he had never seen till he took up his position for the attack, 'was such that no personal observation could be obtained of the progress of the attack'.[51]

Higher command, however, made no allowances. Haig's chief of staff wrote to Rawlinson pointing out that 'the C in C did not consider the withdrawal from Contalmaison on the 7th and the failure of the 38th Division to capture Mametz Wood were creditable performances'.[52] On 8 July, Haig wrote in his diary:

> The 38th Welsh Division, which had been ordered to attack Mametz Wood had not advanced with determination to the attack. General Horne, commanding XV Corps, is enquiring into General Philipps's conduct as divisional GOC. The artillery preparation was...reported as 'highly satisfactory'...[53]

Rawlinson was also disappointed. 'A day of heavy fighting without very much success,' he wrote in his journal on the evening of the 7th. 'We took Contalmaison in the morning but failed to get into Mametz Wood. Prisoners tell us the Boche are in a state of chaos but their machine gunners seem to go on fighting all right. In the pm we lost Contalmaison without sufficient excuse I think as it is reported we were shelled out. I have orded both attacks to be renewed. It is raining hard tonight. We must go on pressing the Boche now they are getting tired as fresh troops may be brought up...'[54]

8-9 July

On 8 July, the 17th Division continued to hammer away at Quadrangle Support trench, again without success although it mounted two full-scale attacks during the day. The 38th Division was ordered to make a quiet raid during the night of 7th/8th on 'something like a company front, not necessarily by the whole company'. 'The place,' said XV Corps, 'must be chosen by the commander of the 113th Brigade now holding the line, who should carry out the raid and fix the exact point. Neither corps nor division, not being on the spot, could fix this.'[55] Shortly after midnight, corps learned that Brig.-Gen. Price-Davies (113th Brigade) was preparing to make an attack on Strip Trench using a whole battalion. Horne immediately telephoned 38th Division headquarters to say that what he wanted that day was a small scale probe of the southern defences and not 'an isolated attack by one battalion on point H'.[56] A few hours later he went over to 38th Division headquarters to discuss the situation and then ordered a night attack on Strip Trench to be exploited the following day.[57] This attack, timed for 2 am, failed to materialise. Corps demanded to know why and so did Fourth Army; division asked brigade. Brigade said that orders arrived at the battalion too late to be executed, the 14th Royal Welsh Fusiliers having reported by orderly that trenches leading to the starting point of the attack had been so congested that they had failed to get there in time.[58]

This was too much for Lt.-Gen. Horne. When Haig and Rawlinson visited XV Corps on the 9th, he told them that he 'was very disappointed with the work of the 17th Division (Pilcher) and 38th Division (Philipps)'. 'Both these officers have been removed,' Haig wrote in his diary that evening. 'In the case of the latter division although the wood had been most adequately bombarded [on 7 July], the division never entered the wood, and in the whole division the total casualties for the 24 hours was under 150.'[59]

Maj.-Gen. Philipps had in fact received his marching orders at 11 o'clock that morning. At the suggestion of Fourth Army headquarters, Horne decided to put the 38th Division temporarily under the command of Maj.-Gen. Watts, commander of the 7th Division, then in reserve. Watts was given freedom to 'dispose of the 38th Division as he wished, keeping any brigades he wanted, or using them as required'.[60]

News of Ivor Philipps's removal soon reached Lloyd George, the new Secretary of State for War, in London. He wrote to his brother, William George, on 11 July giving tidings of the division, which, he said, was doing 'brilliantly'. 'Unfortunately,' he wrote, 'the general has broken down in health and he returned home last night bringing with him his ADC Lieut. Gwilym Lloyd George.'[61]

With this cloud hanging over it, and with a new general and his staff in command, the 38th (Welsh) Division prepared for its next attack on Mametz Wood.

MAMETZ
ILLUSTRATIONS

1. Lt. Bracher with the first ten recruits to the 16th (Cardiff City) Bn at Porthcawl Beach, August/September 1914.

2. Captain (later Lt. Col.) Frank Gaskell with Glamorgan Constabulary recruits for the 16th (Cardiff City) Bn. Gaskell was the battalion's first Commanding Officer.

3. Mametz Wood from the 'cliff' as it is today.

4. Mametz Wood, July 1916,
showing undergrowth.

5. German observation post in Mametz Wood.

6. German soldiers captured in the Battle for Bazentin Ridge being marched away in the Fricourt area, 14 July 1916.

7. Memorial to the 38th (Welsh) Division facing Mametz Wood, 1987.

4. Mametz Wood, 9-12 July 1916.

And to your front, stretched long laterally,
and receded deeply,
the dark wood.

9 July

In the early hours of 9 July, 38th Division headquarters, then still under the command of Ivor Philipps, issued orders for an attack that afternoon on the southern edge of Mametz Wood from White Trench.[1] Two brigades were to take part: the 114th Brigade (Brig.-Gen. Marden) on the right making the main thrust east of the central ride, the 113th Brigade (Brig.-Gen. Price-Davies) supporting with a simultaneous attack by one battalion on Strip Trench. Once Strip Trench and the southernmost cross ride had been captured, the 114th Brigade was to sweep on alone northwards through the wood leaving the 113th Brigade to consolidate the southwestern approaches.

By midday, however, Ivor Philipps had been relieved of his command and XV Corps decided to postpone the attack. It sent the following message to the 38th Division:

> The attack being prepared by you for 4 pm this afternoon will not take place. All preparations for making that attack are to be ready by early tomorrow morning.[2]

The words 'by you' are indicative of a significant change in XV Corps' control of operations. Previously, it had planned each attack itself in great detail. Now it seemed content to lay down guidelines and let divisions work out their own tactics.

Direct orders were now replaced by advice, and in some messages it even pleaded for a particular course of action to be followed. It would be tempting to put this down to lessons learned on 7 July but it is more likely that corps headquarters was simply too busy preparing for the forthcoming attack on Bazentin ridge to spare much time for Mametz Wood.

At 2 pm XV Corps sent a message to divisions urging them not to dissipate their efforts on piecemeal attacks:

> All prisoners captured in the last 24 hours express astonishment that our infantry does not attack in greater strength instead of bombing up trenches in twos or threes. The enemy is much in confusion there being small groups here and there of every regiment. There are some stretches of country without any enemy in it at all. If our infantry attacked in strength they could sweep the whole of them back...All communications trenches to the rear are smashed. This information confirms that already received from aircraft and other sources. Corps commander impresses on all commanders the necessity of utmost vigour and determination in the attacks to be delivered today and great results which accrue therefrom. He looks to divisional commanders ensuring his directions on this point are carried out.[3]

XV Corps was, however, still willing to fragment its own resources, and asked 17th Division to have one last fling against Quadrangle Support trench before being relieved in the line by the 21st Division. Corps staff urged a surprise attack that evening using troops that had rested the previous night. 'Machine guns should not stop fresh troops if they mean to get in,' they said optimistically. 'Impress upon your troops that they are going to be relieved tomorrow night, that it is up to them to make their reputation by taking the trench before they go.'

23rd Division (III Corps) on the left had arranged to make another attack on Contalmaison at 6 pm. The 17th could not join in so soon, and in any case preferred to wait for darkness. On the right, as we have seen, the attack by 38th Division had been postponed until the following day. No attempt was made to coordinate the efforts of these three units and the unfortunate 17th Division went into the attack again completely unsupported on either flank.

At 11 pm, the division launched the 51st Brigade against the junction of Quadrangle Support and Pearl Alley, and 50th Brigade against the junction of Quadrangle Support and Quadrangle Alley (see Map 8) as it had done so many times before. After a hard night's fighting the 51st Brigade managed to capture the western half of Quadrangle support but was soon driven back along it to the junction with Pearl Alley where it hung on grimly. The 50th

Brigade, however, was less successful and at 3.30 am on the 10th the attack was called off.[4]

On the right, Maj.-Gen. Watts assumed command of the 38th (Welsh) Division during the afternoon of 9 July. He took with him several members of 7th Division staff including the GSO 1, Lt.Col. Bonham Carter, who was to become the main point of contact between the division and XV Corps. The original staff of 38th Division was not entirely eclipsed, however, and orders to the three brigades continued to be sent out by Lt. Col. ap Rhys Pryce who was also to do good work in the field.

Although Watts had been given a free hand by XV Corps to dispose of brigades as he wished, he decided not to break up the Welsh division but to employ it en masse against the southern edge of Mametz Wood, putting two brigades into the initial attack with the third close behind. In this, he was not departing very far from the plans previously worked out by Ivor Philipps's staff, but by giving the 113th Brigade an equal part to play with the 114th Brigade he much increased the weight of attack and thus improved the chances of success. The artillery programme was, however, considerably revised to make use of techniques developed by both British and French in recent fighting.

Orders for the attack were ready by 5.30 pm on 9 July (see Annex B). That evening, the brigadiers of the 113th and 114th brigade were called to divisional headquarters at Grovetown 'and given orders by a GOC and staff, whom they had never seen before, to capture Mametz Wood at dawn on 10 July, zero hour being fixed for 4.15 am'[5]. As Grovetown was six miles away from the brigade headquarters it was nearly midnight before brigade staffs were fully in the picture. This gave them only three hours at most in which to alert battalions and move them into position, but, in contrast to the situation on 7 July, there had been ample opportunity beforehand for battalion commanders to make a reconnaissance of the approaches to the wood. That evening, corps headquarters sent the following message which was read out to all troops before dawn the next day:

> The Commander in Chief has just visited the corps commander and has impressed upon him the great importance of the occupation by us of Mametz Wood. The corps commander requests that the division and brigade commanders will point

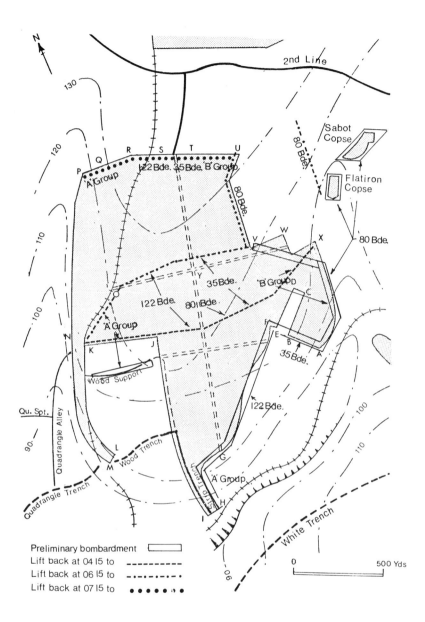

Map 9. Mametz Wood 10 July. Bombardment areas for each artillery brigade and *ad hoc* group showing lift back times.

out to the troops of the Welsh division the opportunity offered them of serving their King and Country at a critical period and earning for themselves great glory and distinction.[6]

The artillery programme apart, there was little subtlety in the plan of attack which relied solely on weight of numbers to overrun the German defences. There were to be no feints, no outflanking manoeuvres: just a straightforward attack in orthodox 'wave' formation across unpromising ground from White Trench south of the wood (see Map 10), down the steep embankment, across the open ground and up a gently rise to the southernmost edge of the wood where the Germans had constructed shallow firing trenches. A distance of some 500 yards of open ground had to be covered. 114th Brigade (Brig.-Gen. Marden) was to attack east of the central ride; 113th Brigade (Brig.-Gen. Price-Davies) on its left advancing on a narrow front between Strip Trench and the central ride. The first objective was the capture by 6.15 am of the area south of the first cross ride and also the Hammerhead. Once in the wood, the two brigades were to keep in touch along the central ride which would be neatly marked with red flags as the troops advanced.[7]

The artillery programme, however, contained two novel features. The first of these had been evolved by the French to draw enemy troops out of of their dug-outs and expose them to shell fire. The technique, which at that time was not in general use on the British front, was to bombard the enemy front line, lift towards the rear as if an infantry attack was about to be launched, and then drop back on the front line a few minutes later as the enemy came out to man the parapets. There were many variants, some including simulated infantry attacks, but the one adopted by the combined artilleries of the 7th and 38th Divisions was as follows. From 3.30 am to 4 am, every available 18-pounder was first to bombard the southern edge of the wood and then 'search' back for a distance of 200 yards. From 4 am to 4.10 am the bombardment would be switched back to the edge of the wood, all 18-pounders and 4.5 inch howitzers firing three rounds per gun per minute for ten minutes and then firing as rapidly as possible for another five minutes before making the final lift in advance of the attacking infantry.

The second feature was the use of a creeping barrage, then in the early stages of development, although it had been tried out

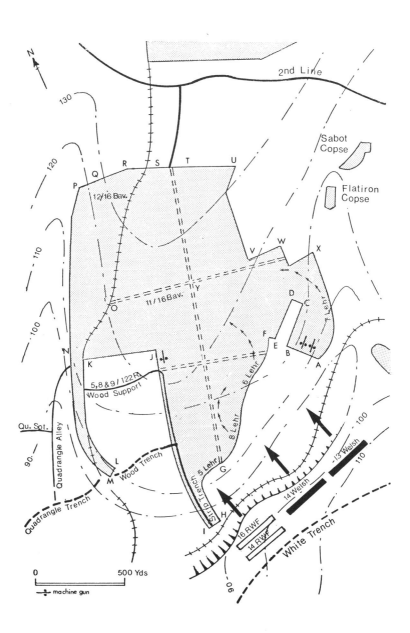

Map 10. Mametz Wood 10 July. 4.15 am.

tentatively as early as the battle of Loos in 1915 and had been used by XIII Corps on 1 July 1916. A barrage, as the name suggests, is not aimed at any particular target but is intended to form a barrier between the attacking infantry and enemy reinforcements. Originally it had been put down well ahead of attacking troops - often on the enemy support trenches - but the advantage of keeping it as close as possible to the infantry soon became apparent. The ultimate development was to move the barriage forward at walking pace with the infantry following very close behind. For the attack on Mametz Wood it was arranged that at 4.15 am the barrage would lift back from the southern edge of the wood by steps of 50 yards each minute to a line just north of the first cross ride and west of the Hammerhead where it would remain until 6.15 am giving the infantry time to consolidate their positions. The barrage was then to lift slowly back, this time coming to rest just north of the second ride. At 7.15 am it was to be lifted again to the northern edge of the wood, and one hour later to the German second line beyond the wood.[8] The bombardment areas allocated to the various artillery groups and batteries are shown in Map 9 which is constructed from operational orders issued by the commander of the 7th Division's artillery.

10 July

Shortly before the attack, 18th Division, on the XIII Corps front, was relieved in Caterpillar Wood by the 3rd Division. This, however, was in preparation for the forthcoming assault on Bazentin ridge; 3rd Division was to play no part in the fighting for Mametz Wood. 38th Division therefore retained a presence in Caterpillar Wood from which to command the eastern edge of Mametz Wood. To the left of the 38th, 17th (Northern) Division was continuing its struggle to capture Quadrangle Support trench. Its role on 10 July was to support the left flank of the 38th Division until relieved in the evening by the 21st Division. Further to the left, on the III Corps front, 23rd Division was to continue its attempt to capture Contalmaison.

As on 7th July, the southern edge of Mametz Wood was held by the 2nd Battalion (Companies 5, 6, 7 and 8) of the Lehr Infantry Regiment (3rd Guards Division). Behind it were units from other divisions including part of the 3rd Battalion, 16th Bavarian Regiment, and of the 2nd Battalion, 184th Regiment. Wood Trench and Wood support were held by the 3rd Battalion of the 122nd

(Wurttemburg) Reserve Regiment (183rd Reserve Infantry Division) which had relieved the 163rd Regiment a few days before. Other battalions of the 122nd Regiment held Quadrangle Support, the Kaisergraben and Contalmaison village.

East of the wood, the 3rd Battalion of the Lehr Regiment continued to hold the German second line from Bazentin le Petit Wood to Bazentin le Grand and also the positions forward of this around Flatiron and Sabot Copses. Northwest of the wood, the second line was occupied by a mixed force of the 1st Battalion Lehr Regiment and the Fusilier Battalion of the 9th Grenadier Guards, both well under strength and badly shaken as a result of earlier fighting in defence of Contalmaison.[9]

With such a mixture of units, and with both British and German battalions at less than full strength, it is impossible accurately to estimate the relative strength of the two sides. One German source[10] puts the ratio of battalions on this part of the front at four to one in favour of the British: three British divisions (23rd, 17th and 38th) of twelve battalions each, against three German regiments (183rd, which was west of Contalmaison, 122nd Reserve and Lehr) of three battalions each, but this ignores the other German units mentioned above and thus overstates the British advantage. It seems probable, however, that the British infantry outnumbered the German by at least three to one. The Germans, of course, had the advantage of being on the defensive in well prepared positions and their troops were in general much more highly trained and experienced in battle. The Lehr Regiment, for example, which was to bear the brunt of the attack at Mametz Wood, had previously fought on the Russian front.[11]

The morning of 10 July was fair and bracing. By 3 am the leading battalions of the 38th Division were in position between White Trench and the brow of the cliff waiting, nervously, for zero hour. They were to attack in parallel lines, or 'waves', as they had practised in manoeuvres, with bayonets fixed and rifles held in the high port position, four paces between each man, 100 yards between each line, the 16th RWF leading for the 113th Brigade with 14th RWF close behind; and the 13th and 14th Welsh, side by side, leading on the 114th Brigade front (see Map 10).[12] David Jones, a private soldier with the 15th RWF in close support on the left in Queen's Nullah, has captured the feeling of tension among the waiting infantry:

Racked out to another turn of the screw
the acceleration heightens;
the sensibility of these instruments to register,
fails;
needle dithers disorientate.
The responsive mercury plays laggard to such fevers - you
simply can't take any more in.
And the surfeit of fear steadies to dumb incognition, so
that when they gave the order to move upwards to align with
'A', hugged already just under the lip of the aclivity
inches below where his traversing machine guns
perforate to powder white -
white creatures of chalk pounded
and the world crumbled away
and get ready to advance
you have not capacity for added fear...[13]

On the left, the 16th RWF sang hymns in Welsh and Lt. Col.
Carden addressed his men with religious fervour. 'Boys, make
your peace with God! We are going to take that position and some
of us won't come back. But we are going to take it.'[14] At
3.30 am the artillery opened up as planned and 20 minutes later
a smoke screen, laid just south of Strip Trench, drifted
effectively north-eastwards. As zero hour approached, the two
leading battalions of the 114th Brigade, having the greater
distance to travel, moved off early, at 4.09 am, so as to be
near the wood when the artillery lifted off the southern edge.
This seems to have taken the 16th RWF by surprise and caused a
moment of confusion. Carden had gone over to the 114th Brigade
staff for consultation and was still away when the 13th and 14th
Welsh moved off. His second in command, Major McLellan, assumed
that Carden had become a casualty and gave the word to advance:

On reaching the brow of the hill, the leading lines saw the
114th Brigade, or parts of it, retiring and they too
wavered. Some went forward but almost all returned to their
previous positions. This was not a headlong flight but was
done slowly and was largely owing to someone who cannot be
traced raising a shout of 'Retire'.
Almost immediately after this, Col. Carden returned and
the advance began again. Captain Westbrooke and Lt. Venables
had shown great coolness in pulling their men together, and

this time the movement was carried out in good order. All the officers state that the advance down the hillside under heavy artillery and machine gun fire was executed with perfect steadiness.[15]

The delay however cost the the battalion the protection of its own artillery, and enemy fire from the edge of the wood and from Quadrangle Alley and Wood Trench soon broke up the formation. Carden, a conspicuous figure with his stick held high, was wounded and fell, but he struggled on to the edge of the wood where he was killed.[16] The two companies of the 14th Battalion RWF following closely behind likewise ran into heavy fire when about 200 yards from the wood. Their commanding officer, Major Gwyther, was badly wounded and Capt. Glynn Jones gave the order to reform in a cutting at the bottom of the cliff. Later he described the descent down the cliff as he saw it from his position in the third wave:

Machine guns and rifles began to rattle, and there was a general state of pandemonium, little of which I can remember except that I myself was moving down the slope at a rapid rate, with bullet-holes in my pocket and yelling a certain amount. I noticed also that there was no appearance what-soever of waves about the movement at this time, and that the men in advance of us were thoroughly demoralised. Out of the most terrible 'mix-up' I have ever seen I collected all the men I could see and ordered them into the cutting. There appeared to be no one ahead of us, no one following us, and by this time it was broad daylight and the ridge behind us was being subjected to a terrible artillery and machine gun fire.

I well remember thinking 'Here comes the last stand of the old Carnarvon and Angleseys' as I orded the men to get ready, and posted a Lewis gun on each of my flanks...Mean-while, men were crawling in from shell-holes to our front, with reports of nothing less than a terrible massacre, and the names of most of our officers and ncos lying dead in front.[17]

On the far right, the Lehr Regiment had placed a machine gun company skilfully on the underside of the Hammerhead (see Map 10) and its fire caught the leading waves of the 13th Welsh (2nd

Rhondda) in the flank as they approached the wood. Sgt. Price described the scene:

> We attacked in a two company frontage, A and B Company 13th Welsh leading, followed by C and D. I was in A Company, No 2 platoon.
>
> We were loaded up with four Mills bombs each in our pockets and four bandoliers of ammunition across our shoulders, which was quite heavy and which made the approach to the wood quite a physical task.
>
> As the barrage started we moved off in quite an orderly fashion...The tension and noise cannot be described, what with the traction of shells through the air and the noise of explosions all around us, it was almost impossible to give verbal orders and we had to rely on hand signals for directing any move.
>
> Men were falling in all directions due to intense machine gun fire coming against us. How we got to the wood I do not know; but we got there and entered it for a short distance before the Germans came at us - head on - and there was quite a lot of action before we were forced to retreat back into the field again, where we got into shell holes or any other form of cover we could get. The Germans followed us to the edge of the wood but as our lines were then able to fire on them they quickly returned to the protection of the tree stumps.[18]

As C and D Companies came forward, a second attempt was made to enter the wood. This was also repulsed but a third attempt was more successful and the 13th Welsh pushed on into the wood.

In the centre, the Swansea battalion (14th Welsh) had the advantage of being protected by others from enfilade fire. The battalion crossed the open ground in perfect formation and arrived at the edge of the wood just as the barrage was lifting back. The artillery tactics here worked well and there were few casualties among the first waves of infantry. The rear waves were not so fortunate, however, and several officers fell, including the second in command and three of the four company commanders. Once in the wood the battalion found it difficult to make progress. The undergrowth was thick and the central ride almost indistinguishable. 'Many of the shells, probably from both sides, hit the trees above us, detonated and caused us more casualties,' Sgt. Lyons of D Company recollected long after-wards. 'Progress through the wood was slow due mainly to German machine gun fire but also to the density of the undergrowth in the wood. This also impeded visibility. It was difficult to maintain our sense of direction but I was helped in this by being able to tell the difference between the sound of our guns and the Germans'.[19]

On the left, the 16th RWF also entered the wood, the bombers successfully pushing up Strip Trench in spite of severe casualties. The undergrowth was not so thick in this part of the wood but British shells had blown trees across the trench and at one point water was pouring in from a nearby pond. One of the bombers, Private Griffith Jones, remembered moving up through the mud:

> I came up against a foot-thick tree trunk. I decided not to go underneath as the mud would be up to my neck so I lifted one leg over it...[I saw] a German behind a bush about 25 yards away levelling his rifle at me. I threw myself back...[and] was hit by a bullet in the leg. Eventually I got up in the mud and felt a burning pain and saw the mud-covered putties red with blood. I took the bayonet off my rifle and using the rifle as a crutch I trudged along back down the trench. When I came to the open I fell down exhausted and was taken away by stretcher bearer.[20]

The 16th RWF was soon joined by the 15th RWF (London Welsh), whom Brig.-Gen. Price-Davies had committed to the attack almost from the outset, and later by two companies of the 13th RWF - the last of the 113th Brigade's four battalions. The Germans were now surrendering in large numbers and the three RWF battalions, pushing out patrols in all directions, were able to move towards the first cross ride, joining up en route with the 6th Dorsets (of 17th Division) in Wood Trench.

At about this time, Capt. Glynn Jones, with the remnants of the 14th RWF still gathered in the cutting below the embankment, saw about 40 German soldiers leaving the wood with their hands up:

> Suspecting a trick, I ordered my men to cover them, but allowed them to approach us. When they got about halfway I went out to meet them, accompanied by a sergeant, and sent

them back to our headquarters. As this appeared to point to the wood being unoccupied, I sent a small patrol to examine it; and then we all moved forward. Crossing the trench on the fringe of it, we entered the wood at the entrance of the main ride, and with two patrols in front advanced up the ride in file, as the undergrowth was very thick.[21]

Meanwhile, on the 114th Brigade front, the 13th and 14th Welsh, now reinforced by 10th Welsh (1st Rhondda), also made progress towards the first cross ride which they reached, and then passed, at about 5 am while the barrage was still falling on it. 'We suffered many casualties from our own shell fire', the 13th Welsh diary records, 'Major Bond being killed. When it was realised it was our own barrage we were in and not that of the Hun, the order to withdraw was given and the battalion withdrew for a time. During the interval we fell in with the 10th Welsh coming up to reinforce and got in touch with the 14th Welsh. Lt. Col. Hayes (14th Welsh) ordered the battalion to dig in along the ride at E' (see Map 10). Hayes had earlier sent a message to brigade headquarters asking for the artillery to be lifted right back to the German second line. Brig.-Gen. Marden relayed the message to the artillery but the request was refused. The artillery stuck to its programme and Hayes was told to strengthen his position and to be ready to advance at the appointed hour. According to the official history, this 'afforded the enemy such a respite that he thought better of evacuating the wood completely,' orders to this effect having been written at 4.15 am by the local German commander.[22]

In spite of this, however, the first stage of the attack had been quite successful. Hammerhead on the right and Wood Support trench on the left were still in German hands, but otherwise the first objective had been captured well ahead of timetable, though at considerable cost. Even at this early stage, seven battalions had been committed. Five of these had lost their commanders, either killed or badly wounded, Lt. Col. Ricketts of the 10th Welsh having been hit several times while bringing his battalion forward in support. Casualties had also been high among the other officers making it difficult to exercise control over the many thousands of men already in the wood. The British High Command was however well content, Haig in particular expressing his satisfaction with morning reports that two brigades had succeeded in entering the wood.[23]

If the fighting so far in Mametz Wood had been hectic and confused on the British side, it was no less so for the Germans. At 4.15 am, as the 38th Division penetrated the southern edge of the wood, the 5th Company of the Lehr Regiment became trapped between the 16th RWF pushing up Strip Trench and the 14th Welsh in the centre. Some of the guardsmen, as we have seen, left the wood and surrendered to Capt. Glynn Jones's group at the foot of the cliff, but others held their ground until overrun. The 7th and 8th Companies, however, under Lt. Pfeiffer, worked their way skilfully back towards the northern edge of the Hammerhead to join up with the 3rd Battalion at Flatiron Copse. The machine gun company at the southeast corner of the wood also withdrew successfully, and although two guns were lost, another three kept up a deadly fire as they moved from shell hole to shell hole back towards the second line. In the centre, remnants of the 6th Company joined up with two platoons of the 16th Bavarian Infantry Regiment and held on until the afternoon, when they too were forced back towards the second line.[24]

At 6.15 am the British artillery began its ponderous programme of slow lifts to the second cross ride, the infantry following closely behind. The Royal Welsh Fusiliers on the left, however, met strong opposition at Wood Support trench and at the corner of the wood - point J on Map 11 - where the 2nd Battalion of the German 122nd Infantry Regiment had its headquarters in a well-defended redoubt. Lt.Col. Flowers was therefore sent forward with the last two companies of the 13th RWF 'to find out the exact situation and reorganise the Brigade'.[25] Shortly afterwards, Price-Davies received permission from division headquarters to enter the wood and together with Lt.Col. Gossett of the Fourth Army staff he made his way up Strip Trench, where he was distressed to see a party of men 'running back in panic'. David Jones, who also witnessed this incident, put it down to lack of supervision. 'Something must have developed, if not into a panic, at least into a disorderly falling back - simply because of not having precise directions.'[26]

Order was, however, soon restored and the two fresh companies of the 13th RWF began to advance through the troops in front of them, one company being given the task of holding the first cross ride, the other of pushing ahead into the wood. When they reached the cross ride, however, both companies became caught up in the confused fighting amongst the tangled trees and little further progress was made that morning.

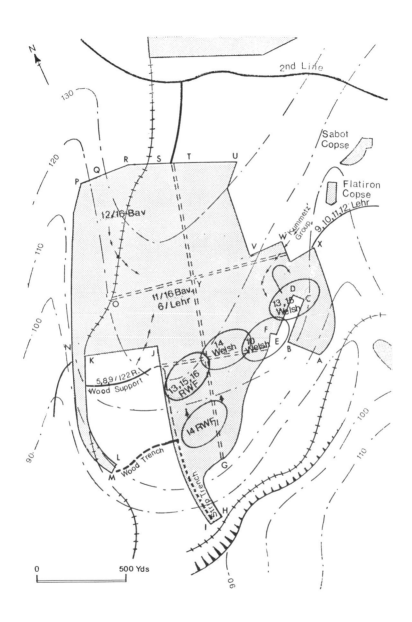

Map 11. Mametz Wood 10 July. 9 am.

Over at Flatiron Copse things were a little easier for the Germans, although the 3rd Battalion of the Lehr Regiment had suffered heavy losses during the artillery bombardment of this area. However, as no infantry attacked followed, the regimental commander, Lt.Col. Kumme, urged the battalion to send help to the 2nd Battalion in Mametz Wood. Major von Kriegsheim, the battalion commander, sent off one platoon each from the 9th, 10th and 12th Companies and to these was added a platoon from the 5th Company, 184th Infantry Regiment. This group, under Lt. Kummetz, reached the eastern edge of the wood at about 9 am, joined up with the 7th and 8th Companies, and created havoc among British troops in the Hammerhead. Later on, Major von Kriegsheim sent another platoon to join this force but only under pressure from his superiors, and even then with great reluctance. He had still not ruled out the possibility that the British might launch a flanking attack east of the wood and he saw little strategic value in weakening the second line at that point.

Meanwhile, as the 13th Welsh on the right was failing to make progress in the Hammerhead, the last of the 114th Brigade's four battalions - the Carmarthenshire (15th Welsh) - was sent in to help. Together, the 13th and 15th Welsh pushed through the Hammerhead almost to point X (see Map 11) but were then driven back by Lt. Kummetz's group which had managed to get in behind two companies of the 15th Welsh and ambush two platoons. Machine gun and rifle fire caught the Welshmen in the rear and of the two platoons (about 100 men) only four men found their way back to the battalion. The 15th Welsh fell back on the line DE, with its left in touch with other battalions on the first cross ride.[27] Thus by midmorning the British line in the wood ran roughly from point J on the left, through F to D and thence in a southeasterly direction to the edge of the wood (see Map 11).

Shortly after 9 am, at the request of 38th Division head-quarters, the heavy artillery had fired for 15 minutes on the wood north of the second ride and on the German second line. But this did not stop German reinforcements from arriving, and large parties of them were seen entering the wood from the north at about 9.35 am.[28] At 10.30, Brig.-Gen. Marden put Lt.Col. Hayes (14th Welsh) in charge of all forces east of the central ride and ordered him to advance to the second cross ride. This he did successfully in the centre, pushing forward about 200 yards before being held up for lack of support on the right.

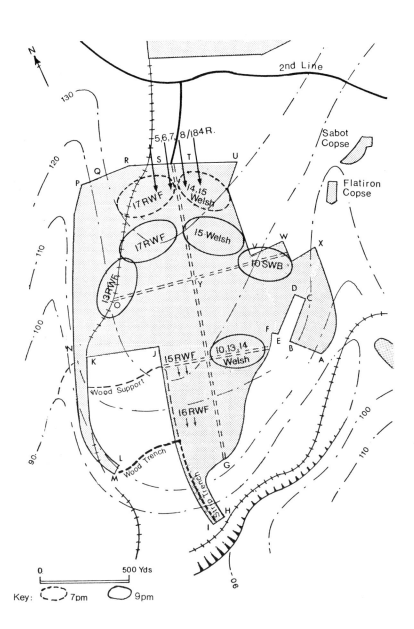

Map 12. Mametz Wood 10 July. 7 pm to 9 pm.

As the wood had now swallowed up all his troops, and little progress was being made, Marden sought permission to enter the wood to see the position for himself and to reorganise. Maj.-Gen. Watts, however, refused to let him go and instead sent in from the 115th Brigade the two battalions that had suffered least on 7 July: the 17th RWF going to the assistance of the 113th Brigade on the left, and the 10th SWB (1st Gwent) to the 114th Brigade on the right. To ease congestion, the 15th and the 16th RWF were withdrawn temporarily from the wood. The fresh troops arrived at about 2.40 pm and gave new impetus to the attack. After another bombardment, the two battalions began to push forward, the 17th RWF bypassing the end of Wood Support trench and the German strong point nearby. To its left, the 13th RWF bombed down Wood Support trench to meet troops of the 17th (Northern) Division approaching from the other end. On the right, the 10th SWB also made good progress, pushing forward to the line YV (see Map 12) with some patrols penetrating almost to the northeastern corner of the wood. Eventually, however, the battalion was brought to a halt by machine gun fire from the northern edge of the Hammerhead.

At 3 pm, Marden was allowed to enter the wood where he conferred with Price-Davies and Lt.Col. Rhys Pryce, the GSO 1 of 38th Division, who had come forward with the reserves. Between them, they decided to straighten out the line and, at 4.30 pm, to make a concerted sweep through the wood. In this attack, the 17th RWF supported by the 14th and 15th Welsh made considerable progress against little opposition on the ground, although German snipers in the trees inflicted many casualties.

By 6.30 pm, the battalion had reached to within 30 or 40 yards of the far edge of the wood. The 10th SWB, which had been tasked with clearing the Hammerhead, pushed between Lt. Kummetz's group and other German forces in the wood. Major von Kriegsheim thereupon orded the withdrawal of Kummetz's group leaving the Hammerhead in the hands of the 10th SWB. On the far left, however, the 13th RWF, which had to spread out westward to cover the wider part of the wood, fell behind and it was some time before it caught up with the other battalions. With the front now close to the German second line, the troops came under very heavy machine gun fire and were withdrawn to a line 200 or 300 yards from the northern edge of the wood, with the left flank pulled back along the railway line (see Map 12). Here they dug in for the night. By now the men were tired and jumpy, as well as being badly in need of water. There was a great deal of wild firing during the night and some men panicked down the central ride when the Germans threatened a counter attack. Eventually order was restored and the exhausted men fell asleep.

During the evening, the German High Command, having completely underestimated the number of British troops in the wood and the extent to which they had penetrated, had ordered the wood to be held at all costs; at 7 pm, it sent in the 2nd Battalion of the 184th Infantry Regiment to recapture the wood, assisted by a company of pioneers hastily converted to a fighting role. Together, the two units pushed through the wood from the north until they met the British troops dug in on a line 200 yards from the edge of the wood. Realising the strength of the opposition, they too dug themselves in.

Outside the wood, the 17th Division finally captured Quadrangle Support trench, but not before Contalmaison had fallen to the 23rd Division at about 5.30 pm. Attempts earlier in the day to capture the trench by bombing up Pearl Alley and Quadrangle Alley had ended in disaster. Lt. Kostlin, in command of a company of the German 122nd Infantry Reserve Regiment holding Quadrangle Support at the time, has described how, in one such attack, the 7th East Yorks, finding Quadrangle Alley blocked 20 yards short of the junction with Support trench, attempted to cross in the open towards him:

> My sentries...noticed helmets moving about above ground level at the sap-head [in Quadrangle Alley] and kept it under careful watch. Each time the men began to climb up out of the sap-head and run forward at us with bombs, the sentries gave the alarm, and we were able to greet them with heavy fire at point-blank range. Then others crowded at the sap-head and repeated the effort, but with equal failure and by midday a heap of British dead and wounded lay about the sap-head.

After dark, however, with Contalmaison taken and the Welsh Division well advanced in Mametz Wood, Lt. Kostlin and his men, threatened on three sides, made good their escape to the rear:

> The ground behind our trench was being continually shelled, but about midnight the fire ceased and we decided to rush for it. The plan worked successfully, and although a number

of men were wounded by shells and stray bullets we
succeeded, a total of five officers and 120 men, in reaching
the barbed wire entanglements in front of the second line
position at 1.30 am. Here we were greeted by a machine gun
which suddenly opened from the trench, but throwing
ourselves on the ground and shouting we soon convinced the
gunner of his error and luckily with no cost to
ourselves.[29]

Thus as 10 July drew to a close, and the 17th (Northern)
Division handed its part of the front back to 21st Division, the
British were established in Contalmaison; in most of Mametz
Wood; and in the trenches in between. Everything seemed set for
for the advance on the German second line. 'Another day of heavy
fighting,' Rawlinson wrote in his journal. 'The 38th Division
succeeded in capturing practically the whole of Mametz Wood and
the III Corps also took Contalmaison. In these circumstances I
have decided to begin the bombardment of their second line
tomorrow and to attack it on the 13th at dawn, weather permit-
ting.'[30] Haig was also well satisfied as he toured army
and corps headquarters that evening. 'I saw Gen. Horne,
commanding XV Corps at Heilly,' he wrote. 'He reported that Gen.
Watts (Comdg 7th Division) had temporarily taken command of the
38th Welsh Division and had nearly got the whole of Mametz Wood.
What an effect on the division has a good commander!'[31]

11 July

At 5 am on 11 July, Brig.-Gen. Evans (115th Brigade) took over
command of all the British troops in Mametz Wood. He established
his brigade headquarters in a shell-torn clearing at the
crossroads on the first cross ride and brought up the 16th Welsh
(Cardiff City) battalion and two companies of the 11th SWB to
relieve units of the 113th and 114th Brigades. The only other
troops at his disposal - the remaining companies of the 11th
SWB, the 115th Machine Gun Company and the 115th Trench Mortar
Battery - continued to hold the western end of Caterpillar Wood.
When he arrived in Mametz Wood, Evans was surprised to find the
front line still a long way from the northern edge, for he had
been under the impression that the wood had been completely
taken, except perhaps for a few yards, and that his task was to
defend it against possible counter-attack rather than to carry
out an attack himself.[32]

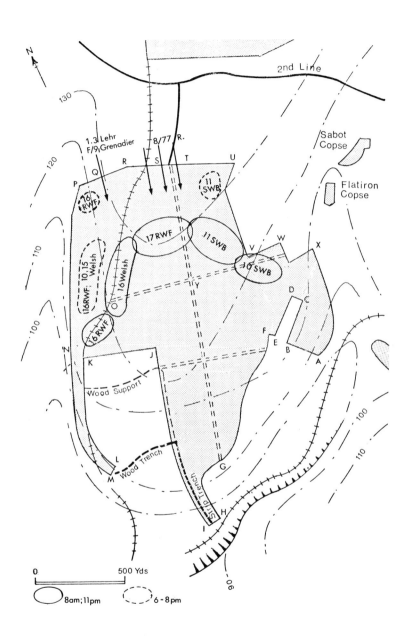

Map 13. Mametz Wood 11 July

When he inspected the line, Evans found the battalions of
the 113th and 114th Brigades, and the two battalions of his own
brigade which had gone into action the previous day, scattered
and disorganised, with some units weak in numbers and very
tired. He therefore straightened the line, sorted out the
battalions, and as far as possible replaced tired men with
fresh. The 13th Welsh and 14th Welsh, in particular, which had
led the attack and been in action continuously for more than
24 hours, were withdrawn from the wood.[33] The new
dispositions were as follows. On the left, the Cardiff City
battalion (16th Welsh) occupied the the line along the railway
as far south as point O, with the 17th RWF on their right
holding the line to the central ride. The 11th SWB held the line
east of the central ride, with the 10th SWB on the far right
occupying the northern part of Hammerhead. The 16th RWF, which
had had a period of rest outside the wood, was brought back to
secure the railway line between points O and K.[34] These
dispositions are shown in Map 13, which shows that in the
centre, the division was still some 300 yards away from the far
edge of the wood.

While this reorganisation was in progress, the Brigade-Major
of 115th Brigade was hit by shrapnel and Evans sent for Capt.
Griffith to join him in the wood. A few weeks previously, Capt.
Griffith had been a company officer in the 15th RWF; now he was
to become a Brigade-Major at the height of battle:

> I passed through two barrages before I reached the wood, one
> aimed at the body, and the other at the mind. The enemy was
> shelling the approach from the south with some determin-
> ation, but I was fortunate enough to escape injury and to
> pass on to an ordeal ever greater. Men of my old battalion
> were lying dead on the ground in great profusion. They wore
> a yellow badge on their sleeves, and without this
> distinguishing mark, it would have been impossible to
> recognise the remains of many of them...
>
> My first aquaintance with the stubborn nature of the under-
> growth came when I attempted to leave the main ride to
> escape a heavy shelling. I could not push a way through it,
> and I had to return to the ride. Years of neglect had turned
> the wood into a formidable barrier, a mile deep. Heavy
> shelling of the southern end had beaten down some of the
> young growth, but it had also thrown trees and large
> branches into a barricade. Equipment, ammunition, rolls of

barbed wire, tins of food, gas helmets and rifles were lying about everywhere. There were more corpses than men, but there were worse sights than corpses. Limbs and mutilated trunks, here and there a detached head, forming splashes of red against the green leaves, and, as an advertisement of the horror of our way of life and death, and of our crucifixion of youth, one tree held in its branches a leg, with its torn flesh hanging down over a spray of leaf...

I reached a cross ride in the wood where four lanes broadened into a confused patch of destruction. Fallen trees, shell holes, a hurriedly dug trench beginning and ending in an uncertain manner, abandoned rifles, broken branches with their sagging leaves, an unopened box of ammunition, sandbags half-filled with bombs, a derelict machine gun propping up the head of an immobile figure in uniform, with a belt of ammunition drooping from the breech into a pile of red stained earth...[35]

Here he found the brigade commander who explained that the battalions were straightening themselves out and strengthening their positions before making probes and reconnaissances to establish whether or not the enemy was holding the northern end of the wood in any strength. Maj.-Gen. Watts at divisional headquarters more than six miles away had no such doubts. He sent a message at 11 am to say that the German trenches in front of Bazentin were being shelled and that 'it was quite impossible that he had any strong force in Mametz Wood'. Watts considered that an attack with only a few men 'advancing with determination' was bound to succeed and he ordered the 115th Brigade to attack and occupy the northern and western edges of the wood 'at the earliest moment', as the corps commander had strongly impressed upon him the importance of clearing the wood without delay.[36] While Brigadier Evans was considering this order, Lt.Col. Gossett of the Fourth Army staff arrived and himself gave orders for the attack to be carried out. 'The brigadier listened to him with the patience of an older man assessing the enthusiasm of youth,' wrote Griffith later. 'When the staff officer had finished, the General spoke. "I've just had orders from the division to attack and clear the rest of the wood, and to do it at once. The defence is incomplete, the units are disorganised, and I did not propose to attack until we were in a better position. My patrols report that the northern edge is strongly held. I haven't a fresh battalion, and no one can say what is the strength of any unit...My intention is to take the remainder of the wood by surprise, with the bayonet if possible; no artillery bombardment to tell him that we are coming. I want a bombardment of the main German second line when we have taken our objective to break up any counter-attack."[37]

When the staff officer had gone, orders were issued to the three battalions in the centre to prepare for an attack northwards at 3 pm, the 16th Welsh working up the railway track, the 17th RWF up the central ride, and the 11th SWB along the eastern edge of the wood. Patrols had suggested that the wood was fairly clear in front of the 16th Welsh but that the 17th RWF and 11th SWB could expect to run into strong opposition. Several German machine guns were reported to be positioned near the centre of the northern edge of the wood.

At a quarter to three, these plans were upset by a heavy barrage put down on the northern edge of the wood by British artillery. As all telephone wires had been cut, it was impossible to stop it although three runners were promptly sent off by different routes in an attempt to get a message through.[38] At 3.30 pm, the barrage lifted - not because the runners had arrived with their messages, but as part of Maj.-Gen. Watts's plan, which had been communicated to 7th Division artillery but not, it would seem, to Evans in the field.[39]

Although the battalions had postponed the attack, they still suffered severely from British shell-fire, as the 18-pounders of the artillery were now firing at the limit of their range and some shells were falling short.[40] When the bombardment stopped, the battalions moved forward. The 11th SWB on the right reached the northeast corner of the wood by 5.40 pm despite stubborn resistance by the Germans, who again made good use of defensive machine gun fire. The 16th Welsh and the 17th RWF, however, met even stronger resistance and were forced back to their original positions. Two companies of the 10th SWB and two of the 10th Welsh were brought forward to help, and the 16th Welsh and the 17th RWF were ordered to renew their attacks to relieve the pressure on the right. The 11th SWB held on to its advanced position and at 8 pm even attempted to work westward along the northern edge of the wood, only to find that the Germans had been strongly reinforced.

The 16th Welsh and 17th RWF were again thrown back leaving

the 11th SWB in a precarious position. Evans, with no other troops at his immediate disposal other than a hundred or so pioneers, realised that units of the 11th SWB were dangerously exposed and, although desperately anxious to hold the northeast corner, he told the commander of the 11th SWB (Lt.Col. Gaussen) to use his discretion and, if necessary, withdraw to his previous position. Gaussen, too, recognised the danger of being cut off, and prudently withdrew. By 9.20 pm all the troops on the right were back where they had started.[41]

Meanwhile, over on the far left, the 16th RWF, now joined by the 10th and 15th Welsh on the lower part of the railway (O to K in Map 13), had managed to gain the western edge of the wood and dig in. One platoon bombed its way northward to come into line with the battalions in the centre, and at one point even penetrated to the northwest corner of the wood. At 11 pm, however, it came under heavy artillery and mortar fire and was compelled to withdraw east of the railway. Towards midnight, the Germans opened up with rifle and machine gun fire from the northern edge, but the British troops were too tired to respond. Throughout the night, the German artillery systematically bombarded the wood with 5.9 inch and 8 inch shells and inflicted many casualties.[42]

The German commanders were determined to hold the remaining strip of wood in order to protect the second line. The remnants of the 1st Battalion, Lehr Regiment, and of the Fusilier Battalion of the 9th Grenadier Regiment holding the line northwest of the wood, were ordered to push forward patrols into the wood, to establish the true strength and position of the British troops. The patrols were also to bring back news of other German units in the wood and, if possible, clear the patrolled area of British troops. These tasks proved to be quite beyond them as heavy artillery fire and difficult conditions underfoot hindered their progress. On both sides of the light railway, they encountered units of the 184th Infantry Regiment in position, but found it difficult to estimate their strength. To the west, but still inside the wood, they met units of the 16th Bavarian Infantry Regiment and sharpshooters from the 9th Grenadiers. They also had difficulty in establishing the extent of the British occupation of the wood but estimated, correctly, that they were within 150 to 200 metres of the northern edge. The patrols failed to make contact with the other battalions of the Lehr Regiment but in the afternoon came across a company of the

77th Reserve Infantry Regiment (2nd Guards Reserve Division) which had been sent forward 'to clear Mametz Wood'. The patrols seem to have regarded this as a futile action, being of the opinion that it would need a large force of fresh troops to succeed.[43] Nevertheless, this unit, together with 2nd Battalion of the 184th Infantry Regiment, helped to frustrate the Welsh attack in the centre of the wood from 4 pm onwards.[44]

Although the German patrols failed to find them, some companies of the 2nd Battalion of the Lehr Regiment were still in the wood, but weak in numbers despite having received a hundred new recruits during the night. The previous day they had lost heavily: one officer killed, two taken prisoner; 82 warrant officers, ncos and guardsmen killed, 61 wounded and 254 missing. The now depleted units came under the command of an officer of the 77th Regiment and continued their stubborn defence of the wood until 8 pm, by which time it was clear that the wood could no longer be held and a retreat to the second line was ordered. The evacuation began as darkness fell and only a few patrols were left inside the wood.[45]

On the British side, four battalions of the 62nd Brigade (21st Division) moved up just before dawn on 12th July to relieve the exhausted units of the 38th Division. This was not before time. The condition of the Welshmen had been cause for concern at corps headquarters as early as 8 am on the previous day, as the record of a telephone conversation between Maj.-Gen. Watts and the corps commander shows:

> 8 am July 11th
>
> The situation in Mametz Wood was being investigated with a view to clearing it up and establishing a line on the northern edge of the wood. General Watts was of the opinion that if the 38th Division was not in a condition to do so, he had better put one of the battalions of the 7th Division in to do the job. Corps commander concurred but impressed upon General Watts the desirability of not using the battalion of the 7th Division if it were possible to avoid doing so. Corps commander would direct GOC 21st Division to arrange with General Watts for the relief of the 38th Division in Mametz Wood at the earliest possible moment.[46]

Later that day, arrangements were made for the Welsh Division to be withdrawn from the battle area to billets around Ribemont and Treux, about nine miles away. The battalions already outside the wood were to begin marching that afternoon. Those still fighting would 'on relief march to the Citadel [three miles from the wood] and bivouac for the night' before proceeding to the billeting area.[47] By the time the last unit left the wood for the Citadel, however, it was 6.30 am on 12 July and there was little time for rest. At dawn the following morning, the 115th Brigade began its long march behind the other two brigades:

> The clear air and fresh sunlight, the green fields, the white road and the pale blue sky all combined together to make a fit setting for a pageant of youth in bright colours. There was a quality in the hour and the place, a harmony in the open countryside, indescribable save in terms of serenity...Against this background of freshness and purity a slow-moving worm of dingy yellow twisted itself round the corner made by a jutting shoulder of downland. The battalions of the brigade were marching in column of fours along the road, and from a little distance it was clear that there was a lack of spine in the column. No ring of feet, no swing of shoulder, no sway of company; slack knees and frequent hitching of packs, a doddering rise and fall of heads, and much leaning forward. Fatigue and exhaustion in a body of men attain an intensity greater than the simple sum of all the individual burdens of its members warrant. This loss of quality in a unit marching away from the Somme battlefield was made more evident by the rising memory of the sturdy column that swung its way down the hedge-bound lanes in the early morning of the end of June, a bare fortnight past, singing and laughing in the happiness of relief from the fetters of the trenches in Flanders. Today the silence was unbroken save by the shuffling of feet and the clanking of equipment...
>
> A walk along the column brought a new aspect of our condition to view. A captain was leading a battalion, subalterns and company sergeant majors were marching at the head of companies, corporals in front of platoons. Men were marching abreast who had never before stood together in the same file. There are no gaps in a battalion on the march though many have fallen, but the closing up that follows losses tells its own tale. The faces of many silent and

hard-eyed men showed they were but half aware of their neighbours, newcomers who jostled the ghosts of old companions, usurpers who were themselves struggling against the same griefs and longings, marching forward with minds that looked backwards into time and space.[48]

The 21st Division had little difficulty in clearing the remaining strip of Mametz Wood. The Germans sent out reconnaissance patrols from the second line, but these offered no resistance and troops of the 21st Division reached the northern edge of the wood just after midday on 12 July. They found hundreds of German dead in the wood and 13 heavy guns.[49] As the Germans had evacuated the wood on the night of 11/12 July however, its capture can be attributed wholly to the 38th (Welsh) Division. It had been dearly bought. The division's casualties for the period 7-12 July totalled nearly 4,000, including 600 killed and a like number missing.[50] Some battalions were severely mauled, including the 16th Welsh (Cardiff City) which suffered more than 350 casualties - almost half its fighting strength. 'On the Somme,' wrote Private Joshua afterwards, 'the Cardiff City battalion died.'[51] On the eve of the battle, the Commander-in-Chief had urged the men of the Welsh division to take the opportunity offered them 'of serving their King and Country at a critical period and earning for themselves great glory and distinction'. Two days later, they had succeeded in driving the Germans from the largest of all the woodlands on the Somme though with appalling casualties. Neither glory nor distinction was noticeably bestowed upon them. Instead they were bundled unceremoniously away to a quiet sector of the front, and took no further part in the fighting on the Somme.

5. Conclusions

...and when the chemical thick air dispels
you see briefly and with great clearness
what kind of a show this is.

The attack on Bazentin ridge

As soon as the 38th (Welsh) Division had penetrated Mametz
Wood on 10 July, Rawlinson made up his mind to attack Bazentin
ridge on the 13th. As we have seen, however, he failed at first
to convince Haig of the soundness of his plan to assemble four
divisions close to the German second line under cover of
darkness and to attack at 'first streak of dawn'.[1] 'On the
afternoon of the 11th,' Rawlinson's Chief of Staff, Maj.-Gen.
Montgomery, wrote afterwards, 'Sir Douglas Haig came down to our
headquarters and we had a tremendous discussion with him as to
whether he would allow us to attack or not. If he had allowed
this, we might have been able to get through the preparations by
the 13th as already arranged. However he still dug his toes in
and it was not until I rang up General Kiggell about 8 o'clock
on the 12th before breakfast that we finally got leave, with
certain qualifications, to make the attack.'[2] This caused
a postponement of one day - a day which, according to one
commentator at least, was to prejudice the outcome of the
battle.[3]

Haig's hesitation is understandable, for the plan involved
great risks. The advance to the assembly positions within a few
hundred yards of the German line was to be made at night across
open ground for a distance varying from nearly a mile on the
right, to about 300 yards on the left. If the Germans were to
discover the plan beforehand, or were alerted by signs of
movement on the night, thousands of British troops on the bare
hillside would be subjected to machine gun and artillery fire,
with little chance of survival. Another difficulty was that
Trones Wood on the right, which should have been captured

beforehand, was still in German hands. It gave the Germans a base from which they could counter-attack the flank and the rear of the advancing British forces. The French could scarcely believe that anyone would be so foolish as even to consider such a plan. When General Gouraud, commanding the French Fourth Army, visited the area afterwards and reconnoitred the ground, he said that 'none of our generals would have risked it, none of our troops could have carried it out'.[4] Rawlinson's staff, however, were completely confident and set about planning the operation with meticulous care.

On the morning of 12th July, the British artillery began a heavy bombardment of the German defences along the three mile front. Because the front was narrower than that on 1 July, it was possible to concentrate the artillery and provide one gun for every six yards of front, compared to one for every 20 yards on 1 July. About 370,000 shells were fired in the two days preceding the attack.[5]

The position of the British front line on the night of 13/14 July, and the forming-up places for the assault troops, are shown in Map 14. From this it can bee seen that the two divisions of XIII Corps on the right (3rd and 9th Divisions) were to be assembled 1,500 yards or so in front of the British trenches in Montauban Alley and well forward of the line in the southern tip of Trones Wood. On the left, the 21st and 7th Divisions of the XV Corps were already established nearer to the Germans, especially the former which occupied Mametz Wood only three or four hundred yards short of the second line. In all, about 20,000 men from six brigades were to make the initial assault on the ridge. At the same time, the 54th Brigade of 18th Division was to attack Trones Wood from the south to protect the right flank of the 9th Division.

After dark, the troops moved forward unobserved by German sentries - even those on the right where the advance was close to the western edge of Trones Wood which bristled with German machine guns. Long lines of white tape guided the troops forward and similar tapes, placed laterally, marked each forming up position. By 3 am - barely half an hour before the attack was due to begin - all six brigades were in place with scarcely the loss of a man and with no serious interference from German patrols.

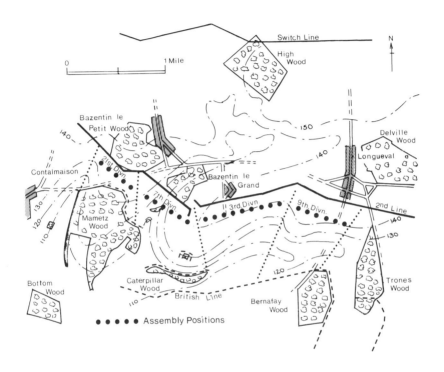

Map 14. Bazentin ridge 14 July.

At 3.20 am 'the whole sky behind the waiting infantry of the four attacking divisions seemed to open with a great roar of flame. For five minutes the ground in front was alive with bursting shell, whilst the machine guns, firing on lines laid out just before dark on the previous evening, pumped streams of bullets to clear the way.'[6]

At 3.25 am the artillery lifted and the 13 leading battalions - no fewer than 12 of them new army battalions - went into the attack. On the left, battalions from the 21st and 7th Divisions entered the German trenches almost as soon as the guns had lifted. On the right, those of the 3rd and 9th Divisions of XIII Corps encountered unbroken barbed wire which they had to cut by hand, or outflank, before they could continue. Very soon, they too had captured long stretches of the German line, except near the village of Longueval, where the 27th Brigade of 9th Division met with fierce resistance. On the left, British troops continued to advance and quickly captured Bazentin le Petit and Bazentin le Grand villages and Bazentin le Petit Wood. The sections of the German line which had so far eluded capture now fell to bombers working round from the flanks. While the main attack went well, the 18th Division in Trones Wood found itself hampered, like the Welsh division in Mametz before it, by thick undergrowth and fallen trees. Not until 9.30 am - six hours after the assault on the ridge - was the wood cleared and the right flank secured.

Although bitter fighting continued in Longueval and nearby Delville Wood, elsewhere the opposition crumbled. The 3rd and 7th Divisions in the centre were keen to push on beyond their objectives to High Wood on the crest of the ridge overlooking the German third line on the reverse slope. At 10 am, several officers walked towards the wood without attracting attention but, in spite of this, Maj.-Gen. Watts (7th Division) was instructed by XV Corps to stay where he was until the 2nd Indian Cavalry Division, which had been ordered up at 7.40 am from Carnoy (four miles away), had taken the wood. The cavalry moved off soon after 7.40 but made slow progress over shell-torn, wet and slippery ground, and by noon was still south of Montauban.[7] The order for the cavalry to advance was therefore cancelled and Fourth Army sanctioned instead an advance on High Wood by 7th Division. For some unexplained reason, XV Corps now preferred to wait until Longueval had fallen. Not until 6.45 pm, after Longueval had wrongly been reported as captured, did 7th Division, supported on the right by cavalry, advance on High Wood from the neighbourhood of Bazentin le Grand. They had threequarters of a mile to cover. At first the going was easy but as they approached the wood the Germans mounted a strong counter-attack from the west, which, though repulsed, prevented the 7th Division from entering the wood until 8.40 pm.[8] Once inside the wood, the British troops moved forward almost unopposed until they reached the German 'Switch Line' running through the northern corner (see Map 14), which was strongly defended. They dug themselves in on a line running through the centre of the wood where they remained throughout the night.

Outside the wood, the cavalry reached the high ground between the wood and Longueval, but failing light soon brought all movement to a halt. In the morning they were relieved by infantry.

During the night, the Germans strengthened the Switch Line and brought forward reserves.[9] On 15 July they counter-attacked fiercely in High Wood and Lt.-Gen. Horne ordered 7th Division to withdraw completely from the wood. At this point, the momentum of Rawlinson's boldly conceived attack was lost, never to be regained. High Wood remained for two more months in German hands. From that time forward, the Battle of the Somme degenerated into a battle of attrition.[10]

Lt.Col. J H Boraston, co-author with George A B Dewar of *Sir Douglas Haig's Command*, had no doubt where the fault lay: with the 38th (Welsh) Division for failing to 'secure' Mametz Wood at an early date. Writing in 1919, he said:

The days lost here were of the greatest value to the enemy. They gave him the opportunity he needed to restore order among his defeated battalions, to bring up fresh troops and to reorganise his defences. Though he could not prevent us from carrying his second line system in our next assault, he was enabled so to strengthen his last remaining defences on the crest and reverse slopes of the ridge beyond that our advance was held up there when within measurable distance of effecting an actual breakthrough.

There is little risk of exaggerating the effect of three days' delay at this stage of the battle, when every hour was of importance. To be seen in the right perspective the incident must be viewed from the standpoint of July 14, when a most brilliant operation came within an ace of achieving great victory...On July 14 our troops broke through the last complete defence line and at High Wood reached the crest of the ridge overlooking the half-finished line running through Flers. For a moment it seemed as though the German front would be completely pierced. Certainly, could our hold on the ridge have been extended to the east where our cavalry endeavoured to push their way forward, and could High Wood have been finally cleared and held, an attack on the Flers line could have been pressed on with excellent chances of breaking through to the open country. The narrowness of the margin by which the German line was saved at this point is the measure of the value of the days lost at Mametz Wood...

High Wood, situated on the very crest of the ridge, represented an advance of two miles from our old positions. Held by our troops, it threatened the safety of the whole German battle line, opening out to us the slopes and spurs falling away northwards to the eastern arm of the upper Ancre valley, with Bapaume and the Loupart Wood on the rising ground beyond. But the opportunity had come too late. Through the northern corner of the wood and along the high ground to the east and west there now stretched Switch lines which barred the passage of our troops, while the gathering strength of the enemy's reserves showed itself in counter-attacks of increasing violence and determination. After holding High Wood for a night and a day, our troops were withdrawn a distance of about a mile to the general line of the Longueval-Bazentin road. Though by the end of the month we had again worked our way forward to the southern point of the wood, it was not until September 15, two months after we first entered it, that the wood was gained and the crest with it.

In the course of those two months, trench systems, switch lines, strong points, and belts of wire were multiplied across the whole space from High Wood to Bapaume. That was a part of the price paid for the check at Mametz Wood.[11]

Boraston does not mince his words. The British Army, he is saying, would have penetrated to Flers and the open country beyond if the 38th (Welsh) Division had shown more determination at Mametz Wood. In other words, he blames the Welsh division alone for the failure of the British army to achieve a 'great victory' during this phase of the Battle of the Somme. This is a serious charge, but is it fair?

Setting on one side, for the moment, the argument that the Battle of the Somme - other than as a battle of attrition - was doomed to failure before it began, it is worth examining the course of events from 1 to 14 July to see if those at Mametz Wood were of special significance and, if so, whether anything could, or should, have been done to speed up the capture of the wood.

The Welsh division took five days to capture Mametz Wood. It took over the line below the wood on the night of 5/6 July and was ordered to attack on the 7th. The attack failed and was not remounted in any strength until 10 July, when the division entered the wood and, after two days of bitter fighting, forced the Germans to withdraw. Boraston's criticisms relate to the events preceding 10 July for he judges the final attack a success and talks of three days' delay, rather than five. Referring to the attack on 7 July, he says:

> In the centre, however, the attack of the 38th Division on Mametz Wood failed, the advance of the 17th Division on their left was swept by fire from Mametz Wood and held up, and, lacking support on their right, the 23rd Division were later in the day forced back from Contalmaison. The 38th Division were ordered to repeat their attack on the afternoon of July 7 and again on the morning of the 8th, when the 17th also attacked; but the situation at Mametz Wood remained unchanged. Further orders were given to the 38th Division to gain a footing in Mametz Wood on the afternoon of the 8th and to exploit their gains on the morning of the 9th. No attack took place, and the 23rd Division, who on that afternoon had again succeeded in entering Contalmaison, were for a second time unable to maintain their position.[12]

Not only did 38th Division fail to capture Mametz Wood during this period, Boraston says, but its failure to do so made it impossible for the 23rd Division to hold on to Contalmaison. Boraston implies, in effect, that Contalmaison could not be held against a German counter-attack unless Mametz Wood was also in British hands. But a glance at Map 4 soon demolishes this argument, or shows at least that it was not a view held by the British High Command. The British objectives for 1 July had included Contalmaison village but not Mametz Wood. And, as the battle developed during the succeeding two or three days, the possession of Contalmaison village was seen as necessary to ensure that Mametz Wood could be held, not the other way around. 'Contalmaison is of such importance to the secure possession of Mametz Wood that it must be captured and held,' Kiggell wrote on 8 July.[13] Nor did Rawlinson believe that the 38th Division were responsible for the 23rd Division's withdrawal from

Contalmaison. 'In the pm,' he wrote in his journal on 7 July, 'we lost Contalmaison without sufficient excuse I think as it is reported we were shelled out.'[14] Thus, whatever failures there may have been on the part of the 38th (Welsh) Division during its first few days of fighting, the division cannot justly be accused of prejudicing the capture of Contalmaison village.

But there are also flaws in Colonel Boraston's main criticism. If a delay of three days in the capture of Mametz Wood had such a crucial effect on the course of the war, why was no attack mounted until 7 July? Why are the three days singled out by Boraston more important than any of the other 11 days which lapsed between the opening of the Battle of the Somme on 1 July and the attack on Bazentin ridge on the 14th?

As we have seen, on 1 July the 7th Division broke through Mametz village and by the evening of the 2nd was in possession of White Trench just south of Mametz Wood. Writing in 1930 of these events, a staff officer of the 7th Division recalled a feeling at 7th Division headquarters that 'a great opportunity was being let slip on the evening of 1 July,' a feeling which, he said, was shared by troops in the front line:

> After the fall of Mametz (by 6 pm on 1 July) the enemy's resistance had been well broken on the front of 30th, 13th and 7th Divisions. Certain localities outside the final objective could have been captured with very small loss, which subsequently were very costly to take.
>
> The most notable of these were Mametz Wood and Caterpillar Wood. To my certain knowledge there were hardly any of the enemy in the former at this time: our infantry in Bunny Alley and White Trench were very keen to push on, but right up to the time of the division relief on 6 July no concerted forward move on [XV] Corps front was permitted, other than by patrols...
>
> An advance by 17th Division through 7th Division from the south against Mametz Wood could have been undertaken at dawn on 2 July, as the whole front here was stable, and defined, by 6 pm on 1 July. Moreover the capture of Mametz Wood by that division in conjunction with an advance by [III] Corps on the left, would have facilitated and shortened the operations which were so long drawn out and costly, subsequently undertaken to capture Contalmaison and the area

between that village, Mametz Wood itself and Fricourt Farm. Had this been done German reinforcements could have been prevented from trickling down to this area.[15]

The official history also echoes this theme of lost opportunities during the early days of the battle. 'XV Corps headquarters,' the history records, 'had received many reports to show that on its front the enemy had not yet rallied, and at 3 pm [on 3 July] patrols found that Mametz Wood and Quadrangle Trench were empty.'[16] The account goes on to say that, at about 5 pm, Lt.-Gen. Horne, the corps commander, gave permission for the 7th Division to occupy the southern edge of Mametz Wood after dark and also Strip Trench, Wood Trench and the eastern end of Quadrangle Trench. Needless to say, if these formidable defences had been taken at this earlier stage, Mametz Wood would have fallen much more easily than it subsequently did and the Welsh division, and more particularly the 17th (Northern) Division on its left, would have been spared much bloodshed. However, the guide sent to bring forward the two battalions of the 7th Division for this purpose (the 2nd Royal Irish and the 1st Royal Welsh Fusiliers) 'went astray' and dawn broke before the troops were ready to advance. 'It would appear,' says the official history, 'that if the XV Corps had encouraged more vigorous action on the afternoon of the 3rd, a hold on Mametz Wood could have been secured, and Wood Trench and Quadrangle Trench occupied. The last named objective was taken on the morning of the 5th, but the others were to cost many lives and much precious time.'[17]

Three days could also have been saved if the attack on Bazentin ridge had been launched on the morning of 11 July when the 38th Division had captured all but the most northerly strip of Mametz Wood and was badly in need of relief. An attack at this moment would have caught the Germans at a time when they were particularly vulnerable and were desperately moving troops out of the second line at Bazentin le Petit to defend Mametz Wood. The British Fourth Army, however, was not yet ready for an attack. Haig was still brooding over Rawlinson's plans and the artillery had yet to destroy the barbed wire in front of the German second line, a task which was not in fact completed in time for an attack on the 13th, let alone the 11th.[18] It was this lack of continuity in British operations more than anything else which gave the Germans ample opportunity to mend their broken fences and bring forward their reserves. And if, as Boraston not unreasonably suggests, 'every hour was of importance' to the achievement of victory, Rawlinson need not even have waited until 11 July. As we have seen, as early as 9 July he had doubts about having to wait for the capture of Mametz Wood before launching his attack against the ridge. There was, of course, a grave risk of a counter-attack against the left flank if Mametz Wood was not secure, but it was a risk he took at Trones Wood on the right flank on 14 July, and which he would have been justified in taking on the left if he had thought it would make the difference between ultimate victory and failure.

It seems, therefore, that Boraston has done the 38th Division a grave injustice, motivated, perhaps, by his evident dislike of Lloyd George, which comes out so clearly in his book. Whether or not its performance at Mametz Wood was all that it should have been - and we shall examine that in a moment - it is not fair to blame the division for the subsequent failure of the British army to break the German line and sweep through to victory. There would have to be something very wrong with British plans if a check - avoidable or otherwise - to one division, out of a total of some 24 divisions[19] engaged in the operations up to that time, could have prejudiced the main stroke.

Views on the 38th Division
But if Colonel Boraston's extreme arguments are easily demolished, the question still remains: was the performance of the Welsh division at Mametz Wood creditable or not? Colonel Boraston is not the only critic. There were some nearer at hand in the division itself.

Price-Davies, commanding the 113th Brigade, frankly admitted that because of his own inexperience, communications within his brigade were practically non-existent, as was liaison between his own headquarters and other brigades. Writing after the war, he said:

> I was as much to blame as those on my flanks, probably more, as I had not been engaged in fighting when the brigade went into the line.
>
> I give only one instance. It must have been on 7 July when

I was visiting my forward posts and looked down on Mametz Wood at a few hundred yards' range. I was by a Lewis gun post when I became aware of an attack in progress by what I believe were the 6th Dorsets [of 17th Division, then attacking Mametz Wood from the west while the Welsh division's 115th Brigade was attacking from the east]. They were creeping forward and using rifle grenades against the strip of wood jutting out towards us. I had never heard of this attack and got covering fire to work as quickly as possible, but the Lewis gun jammed and the attack fizzled out... We occupied a position from which very heavy covering fire could have been brought to bear had this been organised.[20]

Price-Davies was also disappointed with the performance of his own troops when their turn came to attack on 10 July. A few days after the wood had been captured, and the men withdrawn from it, his brigade major delivered this assessment to the brigade commanders:

After a careful consideration of the accounts of the action the brigadier general commanding has the following remarks to make on the events of 10 July and the night of 10th/11th.

The initial advance against the wood appears to have been carried out with the utmost gallantry by all ranks in the face of a heavy fire from artillery and small arms. After the wood was entered, however, and certainly by the time the first objective was reached the sting had gone from the attack and a certain degree of demoralisation set in. The desire to press on had vanished and it was only by the utmost strenuous efforts on the part of a few officers that it was possible to make progress.

The demoralisation increased towards evening on the 10th and culminated in a disgraceful panic during which many left the wood whilst others seemed quite incapable of understanding, or unwilling to carry out the simplest order. A few stout-hearted Germans would have stampeded the whole of the troops in the wood.

Later in the night, rapid fire was opened on the slightest alarm and several of our men were hit and one officer was killed by this indisciplined action.

The brigadier general commanding wishes all credit given for the early success but thinks we should recognise and face our failures...[21]

Battalion commanders in the 113th Brigade were later told to instil in their men 'that the word "retire" is not to be used and that any man using it is liable to be shot on the spot. Officers must deal with all cases of indiscipline of this nature which can only be stamped out by the most drastic action.'[22]

In his report to divisional headquarters, Price-Davies continued this line of criticism of the battalions under his command but he had second thoughts when he heard of the difficulties others had encountered in Trones Wood and High Wood; difficulties which were similar to those experienced by his own troops in Mametz Wood:

> [My report] was made up after the receipt of the accounts furnished by battalion commanders and from my own personal experience. Since then, however, I have had the accounts of certain gallant actions performed by officers and other ranks, and I feel that possibly I may not have given my brigade full credit for what they did in Mametz Wood.
>
> This is probably in great part due to the painful impression left on Lt.Col. Bell and myself (the two senior officers and the only regular officers of the brigade who witnessed the fight and did not become casualties) by the discreditable behaviour of the men of the division who fled in panic at about 8.45 pm on 10 July.
>
> The result has been that the initial success of entering the wood in the face of heavy artillery and small arm fire has not been brought to notice sufficiently.
>
> I feel that some brigadiers would have made a very readable story with the material available. They would, no doubt, have dwelt upon the capture of guns in the wood, and on the number of machine guns to our credit, as well as upon the difficulties of attacking through a thick wood in the face of snipers and machine guns.

Even so, Price-Davies is sparing in his praise: ·

Though I deprecate all forms of bragging and consider that

when failure is disclosed it should be faced, I think it is possible that a certain amount of praise, in fact making the most of such successes as we obtain, is good for morale and improves the confidence and self-respect of the men.[23]

Capt. Glynn Jones of the 14th RWF, one of Price-Davies's battalions, also thought there was little to be proud of during the fighting in the wood. It was, he wrote afterwards, 'nothing less than a glorious mess, from which only the few remaining pawns in the game returned with glory'.[24]

But the most telling criticism of all is contained in some notes compiled by Major G P L Drake-Brockman in 1930, well after the heat of events.

Drake-Brockman was a regular soldier and staff officer who transferred from 7th Division headquarters to 38th Division head-quarters on 8 July and who was therefore in a position to observe the performance of the Welsh division with the eye of a newcomer detached from the field of battle. He found little fault with the fighting troops whom he describes as 'really good material' but he was appalled at the way the division was being run:

> The 38th Division suffered from having a number of senior officers who owed their appointments to their political positions or to being friends of Mr Lloyd George. I can quote two glaring examples...
> *Major-General Philipps.* Was appointed to the command of the division in early 1915, when it was formed. He had originally been a regular soldier but had retired before the war, and at the time hostilities started was a major or lieut.colonel in the Pembrokeshire Yeomanry, and a Member of Parliament. He was thus promoted over the heads of many more senior and meritorious officers.
>
> As a divisional commander it is hardly surprising that he was ignorant, lacked experience and failed to inspire confidence.
> *Lieut.Colonel David Davies OC 16th RWF* [sic]. A politician pure and simple who knew nothing about soldiering before the war: his chief claim to fame was that he had subscribed much money to Mr Lloyd George's Liberal party fund.
>
> It is therefore not to be wondered at that an influential

political atmosphere permeated the whole division and was in some cases the cause of considerable friction. Brigadiers found it difficult to get rid of officers who were useless, since...they were often the constituents or political supporters of the divisional commander, who held a high opinion of their capabilities.[25]

Fortunately, according to Drake-Brockman, the GSO 1 of the division, Lt.Col. ap Rhys Pryce, was a very capable officer 'who in reality commanded the division himself', and there were some 'excellent' battalion commanders - mainly those from the Indian Army.

With Ivor Philipps in command it was hardly surprising, in Drake-Brockman's view, that the division 'did not distinguish itself in its first engagement, though later in the war, under different commanders, it did extremely well'. Ivor Philipps is criticised by Drake-Brockman for carrying out piecemeal attacks, one brigade at a time, and for making it known beforehand that he did not wish attacks pressed home in the face of machine gun fire. In such circumstances, battalions were instructed to return to the starting line until another artillery bombardment had been carried out. Summing up the consequences of Philipps's command, Drake-Brockman says:

By the time, therefore, that General Watts took over command of the division on 9 July, it is not to be wondered at that the infantry were considerably discouraged and exhausted after three days' fighting of this nature.

Conversely these half-hearted attacks encouraged the enemy considerably so that instead of evacuating Mametz Wood as he appears to have intended, he kept reinforcing his troops in the wood.

This, coupled with the thick and impenetrable nature of the wood rendered the final attack a very much more formidable affair than it would have been three days earlier - in fact Mametz Wood on 10 July was a really tough proposition and the division deserves credit for what it did do after being "messed about" for three days.

This, as we have seen, is the interpretation which both Haig and Rawlinson placed on events at Mametz Wood: that under Ivor

Philipps the Welsh division lacked guts and determination but responded well to a new commander.

Drake-Brockman also tells a story of the recall to England of Lt.Col. David Davies and two other officers at the request of Lloyd George who sent a personal telegram to Ivor Philipps a short time before the division went into action:

> There can only be one reason for the recall of these officers and it was certainly a widespread impression in 38th Division at the time - namely that from a political point of view their lives were too valuable to be lost.
>
> I mention this incident because I think it must be almost a record instance for political interference and dishonesty with the fighting portion of the army in France. Particularly is it an illustration of the disadvantages under which the 38th Division functioned, which in no small measure accounts for the very poor performance put up by it during the period under review. Consequent to the elimination of this political atmosphere under the leadership of Major-General Blackadder the division did extremely well during the rest of the war. I served with the 38th Division for ten months, but for the whole of this period the stigma of Mametz Wood stuck to the division and it was common talk in the British Expeditionary Force that 38th Division had "bolted" and the fact remains that 38th Division was never employed again on the Somme.

Drake-Brockman was perhaps wrong in thinking that there could be 'only one reason' for the recall of David Davies to England. On 7th July, the very day on which his "Welsh Army" launched its first attack on Mametz Wood, Lloyd George took over as Secretary of State for War and chose David Davies as his Parliamentary Private Secretary.[26] Whether this was because of his value as a political and financial supporter with first hand experience of the army, or whether, as Drake-Brockman implies, it was to save his skin, may never be known. Either way, the impression made on the division would not have been favourable. It is certainly true that the 14th RWF, which Lt.Col. Davies commanded up until his departure, subsequently suffered more than any other battalion from lack of firm leadership. It is, of course, difficult for a second in command to take over on the

eve of battle and this may account for the confusion on 10th
July when, by mistake, only two companies of the 14th RWF went
into the attack, the other two being left behind until much
later in the day.[27] Ten years afterwards, Glynn Jones, a
company commander in the battalion, recalled the inadequate
briefing he was given before the battle:

> Crowded around the door of a dug-out with the CO inside and
> hardly audible we were given some very small prints of the
> wood and what appeared to be instructions. They were verbal,
> decidedly 'sketchy' and to me appeared to be more like
> instructions for a ceremonial parade than an order for
> battle...When I look back at what was intended to be our
> general method of advance I can well understand how it
> developed into what it did...[28]

But the most significant remark in Drake-Brockman's account is
that for at least ten months after the event it was common talk
in other units that the Welsh division had run away from the
battle. It is difficult to tell just how widespread it was -
Drake-Brockman was hardly in a position to know all the small
talk in the BEF - but it certainly seems to have been a view
held in the 7th Division from which Drake-Brockman came,
possibly because it was to the commander of that division,
General Watts, that Price-Davies would have sent his report of
'discreditable behaviour' by troops under his command. Siegfried
Sassoon, who was in the 7th Division, spoke of 'wild rumours'
reaching them of Welsh troops stampeding under machine gun
fire.[29]

That this poor opinion of the Welsh division was not perhaps
so widely held as Drake-Brockman suggests is apparent from the
accounts of other observers who were in the vicinity at the
time. Gerald Brenan, snatching a few days leave from another
part of the front, cycled around the 'back regions of the
battle' and arrived in Mametz Wood a day or two after 14 July:

> Its trees were torn and shattered, its leaves had turned
> brown and there was a shell hole every three yards. This was
> a place where something almost unheard of in this war had
> taken place - fierce hand-to-hand fighting in the open with
> bombs and bayonets. What seemed extraordinary was that all

the dead bodies there lay just as they had fallen in their original places as though they were being kept as an exhibit for a war museum. Germans in their field-grey uniforms, British in their khaki lying side by side, their faces and their hands a pale waxy green, the colour of rare marble. Heads covered with flat mushroom helmets next to heads in domed steel helmets that came down behind the ears. Some of these figures still sat with their backs against a tree and two of them - this had to be seen to be believed - stood locked together by their bayonets which had pierced one another's bodies and sustained in that position by the tree trunk against which they had fallen. I felt I was visiting a room in Madame Tussaud's Chamber of Horrors, for I could not imagine any of those bodies having ever been alive. Yet the effect in its morbid way was beautiful.[30]

This is not a scene which suggests that the Welsh division had 'bolted' in the face of the enemy; on the contrary, it is a picture of 'fierce fighting with bombs and bayonets' the like of which Brenan had never seen before.

Lieut. St H Evans, serving in the 9th Battalion Welsh Regiment, which, as part of 19th Division, was in Mametz Wood on 23 July, was also unaware of any 'wild' rumours:

This spot was lately made famous for all time when it was captured by the Welsh division in which by some stroke of the pen we are not included. Yet we may claim a share as here we are, holding on and in close support ready to move up...In this one-time pleasant wood now largely splintered to fragments with whole trunks fallen at all angles and the ground cratered out of semblance we dig for dear life.[31]

Lieut. Evans was obviously proud of the achievement of the Welsh division and disappointed that his own battalion was not part of it. The signs of fierce fighting in Mametz Wood also made an impression on another officer, Capt. D V Kelly of the 21st Division which had just taken over from the 38th:

On the 13th [of July] I walked over to Mametz Wood to see General Rawlings, who commanded the 62nd Brigade and was in a German dugout on the western edge of the wood...The wood

was everywhere smashed by shell-fire and littered with dead
- A German sniper hung over a branch horribly resembling a
scarecrow, but half the trees had had their branches shot
away, leaving fantastic jagged stumps like a Dulac picture
of some goblin forest...Along the west edge ran a trench,
from the side of which in places protruded the arms and legs
of carelessly buried men, and as our men moved up that night
to attack dozens of them shook hands with these ghastly
relics. All the old 'rides' through the wood were blocked by
fallen trees and great shell-holes, and over all hung the
overwhelming smell of corpses, turned up earth and
lachrymatory gas.[32]

Frank Richards, in *Old Soldiers Never Die*, talks of 'the
ground all around us being thick with dead of the troops who had
been attacking Mametz Wood,[33] and Robert Graves in
Goodbye to All That tells much the same story:

The next two days we spent in bivouacs outside Mametz Wood.
We were in fighting kit and felt cold at night, so I went
into the wood to find German overcoats to use as blankets.
It was full of dead Prussian Guards Reserve, big men, and
dead Royal Welch and South Wales Borderers of the new army
battalions, little men. Not a single tree in the wood
remained unbroken. I collected my overcoats, and came away
as quickly as I could, climbing through the wreckage of
green branches. Going and coming, by the only possible
route, I passed by the bloated and stinking corpse of a
German with his back propped against a tree. He had a green
face, spectacles, close-shaven hair; black blood was
dripping from the nose and beard. I came across two other
unforgettable corpses; a man of the South Wales Borderers
and one of the Lehr Regiment had succeeded in bayoneting
each other simultaneously. A survivor of the fighting told
me later that he had seen a young soldier of the Fourteenth
Royal Welch bayoneting a German in parade ground style,
automatically exclaiming: 'In, out, on guard!'[34]

There is, therefore, plenty of evidence that the fight was
exceptionally hard and it is noteworthy that few, if any, other
actions on this scale made such an impression on the writers who

were to emerge after the First World War.

If some senior officers in the Welsh division were critical of the troops under their command, others were more inclined to praise them. In a special order of the day issued to the 114th Brigade on 13 July, Brig.-Gen. Marden congratulated all ranks on their achievements of 10 July 'when they firmly established the fighting reputation of the 114th Brigade by capturing that portion of the wood allotted to them by the divisional commander, thereby gaining the thanks of the Commander-in-Chief for the performance of a task which called for special effort'. 'Wood fighting,' Marden continued, 'is recognised as the most difficult form of fighting and it reflects the greatest credit on all engaged that at the end of the day all units of the brigade were under their own commanders. The advance to the attack was carried out in perfect order by the 13th and 14th Welsh, to whom fell the majority of the wood fighting, the severity of which is shown by the casualty lists. The 10th and 15th Welsh showed equal steadiness in the advance when called on to support...With such a splendid start, the 114th Infantry Brigade can look with confidence to the future, and with pride to the past.'[35] In his official report of the attack, Marden expressed the opinion that all ranks 'behaved with great dash and gallantry in the face of considerable fire,'[36] and after the war he told Brig.-Gen. Edmonds, the official historian of the war, that the commander of the 14th Welsh, Lt.Col. Hayes, had written to him saying that the officers and men of his battalion fought better then than they did at Pilckem Ridge in the third Battle of Ypres in 1917 'and got far less credit for it' - a sentiment with which Marden said he agreed.[37]

Analysis

The critics of the Welsh division's performance during the period 7-9 July were, of course, unaware of the extent to which the division's headquarters were being directed from above. Whatever Ivor Philipps's shortcomings in the field, he cannot fairly be blamed for making piecemeal attacks 'one brigade at a time' when he was merely carrying out the orders of Lt.-Gen. Horne at XV Corps headquarters. It was XV Corps that decided on a two-pronged attack on 7 July from positions well over a mile apart. Maj.-Gen. Philipps could perhaps have organised more support by the 113th Brigade perched in White Trench and overlooking both attacks but the role of the 113th Brigade, as dictated by XV Corps, was to stand ready to enter the wood by the southern tongue after the other troops had penetrated from east and west. The evidence suggests that XV Corps interfered far too readily in work which should have been left to divisional commanders and spent too little time coordinating their efforts. It may be, of course, that XV Corps was reluctant to trust either Ivor Philipps or the commander of 17th Division, Maj.-Gen. Pilcher, for like Philipps, Pilcher was relieved of his command a few days later. 'After taking the Quadrangle Trench,' he wrote to Brig.-Gen. Edmonds after the war, 'we wanted, I think, two days before attempting a further general advance. Then by orders from the corps, I attacked at about 11 pm [on 6 July] and was driven back. This attack was quite justifiable and the casualties suffered in it were the result of the fortunes of war. The division on my right was in the early morning to attack Mametz Wood. It was about 7 am that I was ordered on the telephone to attack again over an open plain position which I had been unable to get near under cover of darkness.' General Pilcher was shocked to receive this order:

I protested...and begged to be allowed to confine my operations to a bombing attack, but the reply I received was a definite command to make a frontal attack. For several minutes I pondered and once again took up the telephone with the object of informing the corps that I must refuse to carry out that order, and begged to resign my command. Then I thought that the only consequence of such action would be that someone else would be put in my place and would probably carry out the operation in such a manner that far greater losses would be incurred than if I were to undertake it myself, and I issued orders in accordance with the instructions I had received, employing a minimum number of men. If four times as many had been launched the only consequence would have been four times as many casualties. Neither Mametz Wood, the high ground on my right, nor Contalmaison, the height on my left, had fallen, nor indeed were they being seriously attacked and in such circumstances to attack the low ground between these heights was iniquitous folly. Two subsequent attacks were ordered by the corps with the same result.

When four or five days later Contalmaison and Mametz Wood were carried Quadrangle Support fell of itself.

If I had obeyed the corps more literally, I should have lost another two or three thousand men and have achieved no more. I was, as you know, accused of want of push, and consequently sent home. It is very easy to sit a few miles in the rear, and get credit for allowing men to be killed in an undertaking foredoomed to failure, but the part did not appeal to me and my protests against these useless attacks were not well received.[38]

One can only sympathise with General Pilcher and the 17th Division, but it is idle to suppose that the Welsh division could have come to his assistance: it was a mile away on the other side of the wood. Indeed, as we have seen, the Welshmen failed to reach the wood on the day in question because of the deadly sweep of German machine guns across the intervening open ground. Even had they forced their way into the Hammerhead on the east side of the wood, they would still have faced enormous difficulties. The 115th Brigade diary states that 'Owing to the dense nature of the undergrowth it would have been impracticable to have carried out the programme for the attack as laid down by the time given *even had no opposition been encountered'*.[39] Nor did the XV Corps plans allow for any breakdown in communications and subsequent delay in the transmission of orders though this was a common enough event, and particularly important in view of the distance between the spot chosen by the corps for 115th Brigade headquarters and the attacking troops. The Welsh division's task, like that undertaken by 17th Division, was foredoomed to failure.

If the attacks planned for 7 July were, to use Pilcher's words, 'iniquitous folly', subsequent events came near to farce. As related in Chapter 3, XV Corps ordered a raid on the wood during the night of 7th/8th. Brig.-Gen. Price-Davies (113th Brigade), who was given discretion by corps to choose the spot, decided to attack Strip Trench using a whole battalion. Corps immediately intervened, repeating their request for a small scale probe. Lt.Col. Gwyther, whose battalion, the 14th RWF, had been selected for the attack, could make little sense of it all:

I received verbal orders from Brig.-Gen. Price-Davies,

commanding 113th Brigade, on 7 July to attack the salient of
Mametz Wood with the whole battalion at 2 am on 8 July...
Having issued orders for the same, I was very surprised when
the brigade commander rang me up on the telephone on the
night of 7 July and said he had received entirely new orders
from 38th Divisional headquarters to the effect that my
attack must be undertaken with a much smaller force than was
originally intended and which should amount to the strength
of a platoon, including bombers; hastily fresh orders had to
be issued at the eleventh hour and the party started off
down the communication trench leading to the front line and
our starting place, in good time under normal conditions; as
however the communication trench was full of other troops of
our brigade, progress was so slow that I attempted to get to
the position overground, but found that our advance was so
impeded by barbed wire and other obstacles that I considered
it advisable to resort to the communication trench again,
and the result was that the party arrived very late at the
point from which the attack was to be made. Daylight was
commencing, the element of surprise was problematical and I
therefore decided not to risk men's lives unnecessarily and
reported the situation to brigade headquarters. I consider
that with my whole battalion I could have got a firm foot-
hold in the wood...I have never discovered why the bewild-
ering and sudden change of orders on the night of 7 July
were issued by divisional headquarters.[40]

There is no record of what the raid - by less than 50 men - was
intended to achieve, but Gwyther's account gives an interesting
example of the way in which 38th Division's headquarters were
thought to be responsible when they were, in fact, powerless to
intervene. As we have seen, the mishandling of this particular
operation led to the dismissal of Ivor Philipps, though he had
no hand in its execution.

On 9 July, the 113th and 114th Brigades formed up in White
Trench ready to attack the wood from the south. In the afternoon
the order was cancelled by XV Corps and the bewildered troops
were withdrawn to positions behind the broken village of Mametz.
'God knows what it was all about,' wrote David Jones, 'but they
moved you back again that evening to another place of
bivouac'.[41] Hours later they went forward again,

assembling for the 4.15 attack on 10 July, weary through lack of sleep. None the less, when the order to advance was given the troops moved forward down the slope and into a hail of shells and bullets 'with a success that astonished all who knew the ground'.[42] This was all the more remarkable in that many of the troops had been told that they would be practically unopposed, a situation which one participant[43] contrasts with that at Pilckem Ridge a year later when a fully briefed 38th (Welsh) Division fought well alongside the Guards Division and received great praise. For the most part, the advance to the wood was made in good order especially where, as in the centre, full advantage was taken of the new tactics employed by the artillery. But inside the wood inexperience and inadequate briefing began to tell. On the left, far too many troops were packed into the narrow space between the central ride and Strip Trench[44] to provide for the broadening of the wood, to nearly twice the starting width, just beyond the first cross ride. Here the troops were expected to fan out sideways, keeping their sense of direction. 'A beautiful operation on paper,' wrote Glynn Jones, 'showing more text book knowledge than experience, but ridiculous for a wood full of the unknown, and bodies of men completely lost in thick undergrowth and without leaders.'[45] But in spite of its inexperience, and of the ease with which the Germans could reinforce the wood from the north, or from Sabot and Flatiron copses to the east, the Welsh division during the course of the day fought its way a mile forward and by evening was in sight of the northern edge and only a few hundred yards from the German second line. Thereafter the battle see-sawed for another thirty hours until the Germans evacuated the wood and the exhausted Welsh troops were relieved.

What can we conclude from a study of the struggle for Mametz Wood? Firstly, that there were muddles and confusions at all levels of command, though this is not perhaps surprising given that operations on the Somme were on a much larger scale than anything previously attempted, and proper means of controlling the vast forces employed had not been developed. The set piece attacks on 1 July and 14 July, although they may appear clumsy now, represented a tactical advance on 1915, but the fighting in the period between these attacks was far too fragmented and undoubtedly badly handled at corps level. This combination of penny packets, bad tactics and poor control, made success virtually impossible, especially on 7 July. While separate attacks were being launched on Contalmaison, Mametz Wood and Trones Wood, the rest of the British Army stood still. There was little or no attempt made to coordinate the efforts of the units making these attacks, not even at Mametz Wood where two divisions were converging on the same target. On this front too, XV Corps chose methods of attack that had scant regard for the nature of the ground and which resulted in the maximum exposure of British troops to German machine gun fire. On top of this, as the attack developed, orders were issued at corps and divisional level which had no chance whatever of reaching the troops concerned in time. These were tragic failures, the consequences of which still linger on in the maimed bodies of the wounded and in the minds of the bereaved.

But it is easy to be wise after the event and to dissect at leisure decisions which had to be taken hastily in the heat and uncertainty of battle. It is easy, too, to forget how quickly the British army had grown: from two army corps in France in August 1914 to fifteen, less than two years later. Many of the staff were inexperienced and working under great pressure. There was no time to establish mutual trust between corps headquarters and those divisions which had never previously served in the corps, and which were wheeled in and out of battle every few days. 'Our professional officers,' D V Kelly wrote after the war, 'with certain defects and virtues...were inferior to none, but they were totally inadequate, both in numbers and staff experience for the work of handling millions of men. Why should one expect a man who had never commanded more than a battalion to make no mistakes in charge of a division or corps?'[46] The British army fought the Battle of the Somme before it was ready. But war is not a sporting event: commanders cannot make fixtures just when it suits them - they must react to pressure from the enemy and to demands from their allies. Haig, as we have seen, was reluctant to commit his new armies too soon, but, though he treated it with some reserve, he could not ignore Joffre's cry that the French army would be destroyed if the British held back. Though 'idealism perished on the Somme,'[47] and the British army was never to be the same afterwards, it could hardly have been otherwise given the remorseless pressure of events.

Secondly, although it is incidental to our main theme, it is worth pointing out that at Mametz Wood, as elsewhere on the Somme, great damage was inflicted on the German army by the British artillery. This is something which those who argue that German losses on the Somme could not possibly equal those of the British tend to neglect. They point to the unequal nature of a contest between defenders armed with machine guns and attackers moving over the open ground.[48] That is a valid argument, as far as it goes, but it is not the whole story. As we have seen, infantry attacks were sporadic, and though attacking troops had little chance against machine gun fire, they were exposed only for short periods of time. At Mametz Wood, for example, the infantry of the 38th (Welsh) Division faced German machine guns in the open for a few hours on 7 July, and again for a few hours on 10 July. Casualties were very high during these short periods but the Germans suffered without respite from a hail of shells. And although their second line was equipped with well- constructed deep dug-outs, these were mostly used as casualty dressing stations and were not always proof against large calibre British shells. Much of the trench works soon crumbled away and many Germans were buried alive as roofs and walls were blown in on them. Corporal Hetschold of the 2nd Machine Gun Company of the Lehr Regiment has described what it was like to suffer in this way. He moved into the second line at Bazentin le Petit on 3 July while it was being heavily shelled:

A few dug-outs still remained. And now these were crushed in.

In the dug-out in which I was, 100 comrades soon gathered. It was a strong dug-out but after a short barrage it also gave way. First an entrance collapsed and many suffocated. Then a shell landed in the middle and we were thrown hither and thither. As we came to our senses again, there was a dud shell sticking out from under the framework of the dug-out. We all took fright but it did not explode. We breathed again. But then the next followed immediately. A fearful rending, all the candles were out, shouts and groans. I can still breathe, I hear my comrades calling 'The long gallery is smashed in right up to us; we must get out'. I see two boots, pull hard and manage to free a comrade, who was already nearly dead. But we can do nothing for the others; four metres of earth lie on them. I shudder. There is no escape here. As we make for the second entrance, the next

shell smashes it in. We are buried alive. I feel that I can
scarcely get any more air. Then a pioneer calls: 'I will use
a detonator quickly. If it succeeds, we are free; if not,
the end will come quickly.' I call 'Don't use explosives!
Let us try this way first'. There are perhaps five to eight
of us still alive. We scratch the earth down with our hands
and feet. Dead comrades are unearthed. We press close to the
steps. If the earth falls from above we are lost. My hair
stands on end. Then - a shout of joy! A small ray of light
comes from above. We are saved. Now the hole is big enough
to allow head and chest through, and then we are off to the
nearest shell holes.

Only a few comrades are still with me from our company. We
stick together like true brothers.[49]

The British seige guns, too, kept up a ceaseless bombardment of
depots and supply lines to the rear and the Germans lost heavily
trying to get food and water through to the trenches. Wounded
men in the front line cried out with thirst and drank feverishly
from muddy water brought to them at great risk from nearby
puddles. Others left the wood in search of water and were killed
in the barrage beyond. It is not possible accurately to draw up
a balance sheet of the losses on each side at Mametz Wood but
there is little doubt that in its own way the German experience
was as terrible as that of the attackers, and their losses,
proportionate to the numbers employed, just as great.

Finally, what of the 38th (Welsh) Division? Whatever faults
there may have been in execution, there can be no doubting now
the magnitude of their achievement. Map 14 shows all the
woodlands of the Somme. Mametz Wood was the largest and one of
the most easily defended, with the German second line just above
it on the ridge. Trones Wood was in a like position but, though
smaller than Mametz Wood, it remained in German hands until
bypassed by the main assault on Bazentin ridge. Bernafay Wood
and the two Bazentin woods were well forward of any rear
defences and fell quickly as a result, though Delville Wood,
similarly placed, resisted capture for nearly six weeks, falling
to 14th Division on 27 August.[50] High Wood held out for
two months against sustained attacks by a number of divisions.
By comparison, the five days which the Welsh division took to
capture Mametz Wood is creditably short and it is not surprising

that some of the early criticism of the division became muted as the difficulties of woodland fighting became apparent.

The capture of Mametz Wood was not a tidy affair: the fighting was confused and there were moments of near panic with the Welshmen falling back in disarray. Leaderless men straggled out of the wood looking for directions. The performance did not at first sight perhaps suggest 'one of the most magnificent little armies ever turned out' but the Welsh division, inexperienced and inadequately trained, pushed the cream of Germany's professional army back about one mile in most difficult conditions, an achievement which should rank with that of any division on the Somme - including the much vaunted 7th Division.

Addressing reserves for the Welsh division at Kinmel Park in North Wales some weeks later, Lloyd George said:

> You are proceeding to a great struggle. I know the dangers you have to face. You will face them like men. The men belonging to the division you have the honour to belong to are a credit to their race. They had a very difficult piece of work to do on the Somme in that great battle. They accomplished much with honour to themselves and to the land to which they belonged. The attack on Mametz Wood was one of the most difficult enterprises which fell to any division. It was left to the Welsh division, and they swept the enemy out of it. From end to end there is not a living German in the wood now. He has been driven far beyond it, and it will be your task to drive him still further and I think in time you will accomplish it. When I look down upon you I know the gallantry with which your comrades in France have fought, and I bid you God speed.[51]

Stripped of rhetoric and bombast, this represents no more than the simple truth, though it ignores the suffering experienced by both sides. The Welsh division's performance was disappointing only when measured against the unrealistic expectations of higher commands. By any objective measure it did remarkably well.

Notes on Chapter One

Epigraph: David Jones, *In Parenthesis*, London 1937, p.4.

1. Kenneth O Morgan [ed.], *Lloyd George: Family Letters 1885-1936*, Cardiff and London 1973, p.167.
2. *The Times*, 3 August 1914.
3. Keith Robbins, *Sir Edward Grey*, London 1971, p.291.
4. Grey of Falloden, *Twenty-five years*, London 1925, ii, p.177.
5. Trevor Wilson [ed.], *The Political Diaries of C P Scott 1911-1928*, London 1970, p.97.
6. Parliamentary Debates, *Official Report*, House of Commons, 3 August 1914, columns 1809-1827. The quotation is from column 1825.
7. For an account of these reforms see Col J K Dunlop, *Development of the British Army 1899-1914*, London 1938, and Peter Fraser's political biography, *Lord Esher*, London 1973, which gives most of the credit for reform to Esher.
8. *The Times*, 4 August 1914.
9. Parliamentary Debates, *Official Report*, House of Commons, 6 August 1914, column 2082.
10. Philip Magnus, *Kitchener: Portrait of an Imperialist*, London 1958, p.341 (Penguin edition).
11. Viscount Esher, *The Tragedy of Lord Kitchener*, London 1921, p.35.
12. *The Times*, 7 August 1914.
13. C E Montague, *Disenchantment*, London 1922, p.10 (MacGibbon & Kee edition 1968).
14. Communication from Lord Kitchener to the County Associations and officers commanding territorial units. Quoted in *The Times*, 15 August 1914.
15. By analysis from A F Becke, *History of the Great War based on Official Documents; Order of Battle of Divisions*, London 1938.
16. Brian Bond, 'The Territorial Army in Peace and War', *History Today*, Vol. XVI, No.3, 1966, p.160. Bond states

that in the first 18 months of the war, 726,000 joined the territorials against 1,741,000 for the Kitchener armies.

17. Army Order 324 of 21 August 1914.

18. The new armies were popularly known as 'Kitchener's Armies' and were designated K1, K2 etc. None of the armies took to the field as such. Divisions were sent abroad as they became ready and fought alongside regular and territorial divisions.

19. *Statistics of the Military Effort of the British Empire during the Great War*, HMSO London 1922. The information is taken from the divisional distribution charts between pp.28 and 29. For completeness, I have included the Royal Naval division, raised by Churchill although, strictly speaking, it was under Admiralty, not War Office, control at the time. A guards division was added later in 1915 and five territorial divisions were added at the end of 1916. The maximum strength at any one time was 75 divisions (Spring 1917).

20. *Field Service Pocket Book*, HMSO London 1914.

21. The number of Welsh battalions in the new army divisions is taken by inspection from Becke, *Order of Battle of Divisions*. If infantry battalions alone are counted, the figure is 25 out of a total of 360 battalions which is almost exactly seven per cent. If pioneer battalions are included the figure rises to 29 out of 390, or roughly 7.5 per cent. The percentages drop to 6.7 and 7.2 respectively if the London Welsh, who were not recruited in Wales are excluded. The relative size of Wales, in terms of population, is based on 1911 census returns as quoted in I Nicholson and T Lloyd-Williams, *Wales: Its part in the War*, London 1919, p.26.

22. In 1908, under Haldane's reforms, the Volunteer battalions associated with the Royal Welsh Fusiliers and the Welsh Regiment became numbered territorial battalions bearing the regimental name. Those associated with the South Wales Borderers, however, underwent greater change. One became the 'Brecknock' battalion of the SWB, but three others were converted into an independent territorial regiment, the Monmouthshire regiment, which continued to be closely associated with the SWB. At first, the battalions of the Monmouthshire regiment were brigaded together in the Welsh

territorial division but they were sent overseas to join other divisions very early in the war, and distinguished themselves at the 2nd Battle of Ypres in 1915.

23. *Western Mail*, Cardiff, 1 December 1914.

24. Peter Rowland, *Lloyd George*, London 1975, pp.284-5.

25. Morgan [ed.], *Lloyd George: Family Letters 1885-1936*, p.169.

26. C T Atkinson, *The History of the South Wales Borderers 1914-1918*, London 1931, p.69.

27. *South Wales Daily News*, Cardiff, 22 September 1914.

28. A J P Taylor [ed.], *Lloyd George: A diary by Frances Stevenson*, London 1971, p.2.

29. David Lloyd George, *War Memoirs*, London 1933-1936, p.452 (Odhams edition). Lloyd George says that when the proposal came before Lord Kitchener 'he promptly vetoed it. The question was thereupon raised by me in the Cabinet and there was a fierce fight. In the end the cause of the Welsh division was carried.' Lloyd George is not very precise on dates but agreement must have been reached before official sanction was given by the War Office on 10 October, and probably before the newspaper announcement of Kitchener's agreement on 23 September 1914. Some historians suggest that the row in Cabinet took place on 28 October, but that was more probably a row about an Army instruction prohibiting the speaking of Welsh which Frances Stevenson mentions in her diary (although she dates it at 29 October).

30. *Welsh Army Corps Executive Committee Report 1914-1919* (referred to hereafter as *WACEC*), Cardiff 1921, pp.4-6.

31. *South Wales Daily News*, Cardiff, 30 September 1914.

32. *WACEC*, p.12.

33. *Western Mail*, Cardiff, 1 October 1914.

34. ibid.

35. ibid., 14 October 1914.

36. *WACEC*, p.40.

37. C H D Ward, *Regimental Records of the Royal Welch Fusiliers 1914-1918*, London 1928, p.26.

38. Compiled from information in *WACEC* and in J E Munby, *A History of the 38th (Welsh) Division*, London 1920.

39. *South Wales Daily News*, Cardiff, Thursday 19 November 1914.

40. Taylor, *Lloyd George: A diary by Frances Stevenson*, p.8.
41. Morgan [ed.], *Lloyd George: Family Letters 1885-1936*, p.175.
42. Taylor, *Lloyd George: A diary by Frances Stevenson*, p.24. Ivor Philipps took command of the division on 19 January 1915. The quotation is taken from the entry in the diary for 25 January 1915.
43. *Western Mail*, Cardiff, 2 December 1914.
44. ibid., 18 December 1914.
45. *Daily News and Leader*, London, 2 March 1915.
46. *Daily Post and Mercury*, Liverpool, 2 March 1915.
47. *Western Mail*, Cardiff, 2 March 1915.
48. *Carnarvon and Denbigh Herald*, Carnarvon, 5 March 1915.
49. Munby, *A History of the 38th (Welsh) Division*, pp.5-10.
50. *WACEC*, p.25.
51. *Western Mail*, Cardiff, 3 May 1915.
52. *WACEC*, pp.28-29.
53. Guy Chapman, *A Passionate Prodigality*, London 1933, p.13 (MacGibbon & Kee edition 1965).

54. Lloyd George MS. Lord Plymouth to Lloyd George, 13 December 1914.
55. B Williams, *Raising and Training the New Armies*, London 1918, p.69.
56. Richard Lyons, letter to the author, 4 September 1972.
57. V W Germains, *The Kitchener Armies*, London 1930, p.128.
58. *Western Mail*, Cardiff, 14 December 1914.
59. ibid., 16 December 1914.
60. Atkinson, *The History of the South Wales Borderers 1914-1918*, p.177.
61. Lloyd George MS. Owen Thomas to Lloyd George, 9 July 1915.
62. Reported in the *Carnarvon and Denbigh Herald*, 3 December 1915.
63. Ll Wyn Griffith, 'The pattern of One Man's Remembering' in *Promise of Greatness* [ed. George A Panichas], London 1968, p.288.
64. WO95/2540, 38th Division War Diary (unnumbered document placed among papers for December 1916).
65. Richard Lyons, letter to the author, 4 September 1972.

Notes on Chapter Two

Epigraph: David Jones, *In Parenthesis*, London 1937, p.54.

1. Ll Wyn Griffith, *Up to Mametz*, London 1931, p. 12.
2. Jones, *In Parenthesis*, p.7.
3. WO95/2539, 38th Division War Diary. First entry (6 December 1915) and Appendix II.
4. Robert Blake, *The Private Papers of Douglas Haig 1914-1919*, London 1952, p.115.
5. Lord Hankey, *The Supreme Command*, Vol. 2, London 1961, p.444.
6. Philip Magnus, *Kitchener*, London 1958, p.426 and pp. 435-6.
7. Paul Guinn, *British Strategy and Politics 1914 to 1918*, Oxford 1965, p.113. However, Robertson himself, in *Private to Field Marshal*, London 1921, gives no hint of any connivance.
8. Hankey, *The Supreme Command*, Vol. 2, p.466.
9. Cyril Falls, *The First World War*, London 1960, p.84. The official history (1916 Vol 1, p.18) puts the figure at 38, but notes that 'the 46th Division, part of which was on passage to Egypt, is counted as in France'.
10. Victor Bonham-Carter, *Soldier True: The Life and Times of Field Marshal Sir William Robertson*, London 1963, pp.154-5.
11. Hankey, *The Supreme Command*, p.469.
12. Blake, *The Private Papers of Douglas Haig*, p.124. Also Bonham-Carter, *Soldier True, p.154.*
13. *Hankey, The Supreme Command, p.469.*
14. Edmonds, *Official History* 1916 Vol. 1, p.21. The division started to embark on 1 January 1916 but because of a shortage of ships the move was eventually cancelled.
15. Jones, *In Parenthesis*, p.13.
16. WO95/2539, 38th Division War Diary; also brigade and battalion diaries. Appendix VII to the 38th Division's diary for December gives the training programme in full but battalion records show that it was not possible to implement every instruction.
17. ibid.
18. Griffith, *Up to Mametz*, p.21.

19. Jones, *In Parenthesis*, pp.43-9.
20. Griffith, *Up to Mametz*, pp.56-7.
21. Edmonds, *Official History* 1916 Vol. 1, pp.157-8.
22. WO95/881, XI Corps War Diary, entry for 12 January 1916.
23. WO95/2539, 38th Division War Diary. Appendix V to entry for January 1916: Memorandum by Lt.-Gen. R Haking, 'to be read out to all troops in the 38th Division'.
24. WO95/881, XI Corps War Diary. In the Battle of Fromelles, July 1916, intended as a diversion from the Battle of the Somme, two divisions, one British, one Australian, lost heavily in an ill-conceived attack on the German line opposite the First Army/ Second Army boundary. In 1930, Maj.-Gen. Elliott, who had been a brigade commander in the Australian Division, launched a bitter attack on Haking who had been responsible for the plans: 'One general of strong personality and little ability seems to have been allowed to run the battle without control which produced such disastrous results'.
25. Jones, *In Parenthesis*, p.71.
26. WO95/2539, 38th Division War Diary, Tactical Progress Report No.7. Quoted verbatim except that names of the nearest geographical features have been substituted for map references and some repetitive phrases have been omitted. The associated map is based on a section of the Ordnance Survey map for the Richebourg area (Imperial War Museum: Edition 9A).
27. WO95/2559, 14th Welsh War Diary.
28. Griffith, *Up to Mametz*, p.77.
29. Not just in the 38th Division; see, for example, Edmund Blunden, *Undertones of War*, London 1928, p.38 (Penguin edition 1936).
30. WO95/2557, 114th Infantry Brigade War Diary. An Appendix to the May 1916 volume, 38th Division instruction GS13/6/1, dated 22/5/16, asked brigades in reserve to train two companies at a time in carrying out attacks.
31. Edmonds, *Official History* 1916 Vol. 1, pp.25-7.
32. ibid., p.28.
33. Blake, *The Private Papers of Douglas Haig*, p.129.
34. Bonham-Carter, *Soldier True*, p.170; also Blake, p.138.
35. Blake, *The Private Papers of Douglas Haig*, pp144-5. Quoted also by Guinn, p.159.

36. Guinn, *British Strategy and Politics 1914 to 1918*, p.139.
37. T O Marden, *History of the Welch Regiment 1914-1918*, Cardiff 1932, p.379. Also WO95/2557 and WO95/2559.
38. WO95/2539, 38th Division War Diary, Annex to May 1916: Report by Lt.Col. R C Bell, 15th RWF.
39. ibid., and WO95/2551. Lt.-Gen. Haking's praise of the battalion is recorded in a manuscript addition, in his hand and dated 10 May 1916, to the document mentioned above (note 38). His ranking of 22 raids on the XI Corps front is given in a report to First Army dated May 1916 (copy in WO95/2551).
40. WO95/881. XI Corps copy of First Army's GS 360/24(a).
41. See note 24. Part of the 184th Inf. Bde. attacked from Rhondda Sap.
42. Griffith, *Up to Mametz*, p.170.
43. Edmonds, *Official History* 1916 Appendices Vol. 1, p.125: 'Training of Divisions for Offensive Action'.
44. Richard Lyons. Notes written for the author, August 1972.
45. WO95/2539, 38th Division War Diary, also WO95/2562, 11th SWB War Diary.
46. WO95/2539, 38th Division War Diary.
47. Guinn, *British Strategy and Politics 1914 to 1918*, p.135.
48. ibid. In a footnote to page 136, Guinn quotes Liddell Hart as saying that in the autumn of 1915 the defences on this front, where he was then serving, were very weak.
49. Edmonds, *Official History* 1916 Vol. 1, p.35. The phrase 'graceful gentleness' is from John Masefield, *The Old Front Line*, London 1917, p.33.
50. *Army Quarterly*, Vol. 7, No. 2, pp.245-55: 'Other side of the Hill' - an account of German defences during the battle of the Somme based on German regimental histories. The quotation 'tier upon tier' is from Cruttwell, *A History of the Great War*, Oxford 1936, p.259.
51. Edmonds, *Official History* 1916 Vol.1, p.250.
52. ibid., pp. 253-4. Another corps - the XVth - was added to Fourth Army when Haig's more ambitious plan was adopted.
53. ibid., p.266.
54. ibid., p.480.
55. B H Liddell Hart, *History of the First World War*, London

1930 (as *The Real War*), p.242.

56. Edmonds, *Official History* 1916 Vol.1, p.481.

57. Haig MS. Diary entry for 1 July 1916.

58. ibid.

59. Rawlinson MS. Journal entry for 2 July 1916.

60. Haig MS. Diary entry for 2 July 1916. Earlier, Haig had himself visited Fourth Army headquarters to make the same point.

61. ibid. Memorandum from Kiggell to Rawlinson dated 2 July 1916.

62. ibid. 'Notes of interview between Sir D Haig and General Joffre on 3 July at Val Vion.'

63. W B Joshua, letter to the author, January 1974.

64. WO95/5261, 17th RWF War Diary: copy of General Philipps's Order of the Day dated 5 July 1916.

65. Siegfried Sassoon, *Memoirs of an Infantry Officer*, London 1930, p.69. 'Kinjack' is Sassoon's fictional name for his commanding officer.

66. CAB45/189. Notes from J Glynn Jones, captain, 14th RWF, written after the war.

Notes on Chapter Three

Epigraph: David Jones, *In Parenthesis*, London 1937, p.138.

1. WO95/431, Fourth Army Operation Order 32/3/16(G) dated 3 July 1916.

2. WO95/431, Fourth Army Operation Order 32/3/23(G) dated 5 July 1916.

3. Haig MS. Diary entry for 4 July 1916.

4. Haig MS. Diary entry for 8 July 1916.

5. Rawlinson MS. RWLN 1/6, item 87d. Kiggell to Rawlinson, 8 July 1916.

6. Rawlinson MS. RWLN 1/5. Journal entry for 9 July 1916.

7. Haig MS. Diary entry for 11 July 1916.

8. Haig MS. Diary entry for 12 July 1916. An interesting contemporary analysis of the alternatives is to be found among the Fourth Army papers (WO95/431, File A). According to this, the possibility of an attack northward from Mametz Wood was rejected because 'it would be on a narrow front, which two years' experience had proved to be unsound:

moreover, even if successful, the ground gained would form so pronounced a salient that the enemy would probably be able to concentrate such a heavy fire on it as to render it very difficult to hold'.

9. Siegfried Sassoon, *Memoirs of an Infantry Officer*, London 1930, p.64. Sassoon was viewing Mametz Wood from Quadrangle Trench.

10. The figure of 220 acres is an estimate made by *The Times* correspondent in a despatch dated 12 July 1916 and published two days later.

11. WO95/2539, 38th Division War Diary. Appendix X to the volume for July 1916.

12. ibid.

13. *Army Quarterly*, Vol. 9, No. 2, January 1925, p.247 (from German regimental records).

14. Reichsarchivs monograph *Somme-Nord*: Band 20 in the series *Schlachten des Weltkrieges*, 1927 (Maps 27 and 28).

15. *Army Quarterly*, Vol. 9, No. 2, p.248. At the outbreak of war the Lehr (training) battalion of the Prussian Guard - an instructional unit attached to the 1st Guards Brigade - was expanded into a full regiment of three battalions. German regiments, unlike their British counterparts, fought as complete units, three or four regiments of three battalions each in one division.

16. WO95/2539, 38th Division War Diary: copy of XV Corps Operation Order No. 15 (issued at 10 am on 6 July 1916).

17. WO95/ 2539, 38th Division War Diary: copy of XV Corps Artillery Operation Order No. 14 (issued 6 July 1916).

18. Evans MS.

19. T O Marden, *History of the Welch Regiment 1914-1918*, Cardiff 1932, pp.382-3.

20. Evans MS.

21. WO95/2539, 38th Division War Diary, Appendix VII to July volume: 38th Division Order No. 36 (issued at 8.30 pm on 6 July 1916).

22. WO95/921, XV Corps War Diary. Entry for 7.40 pm on 6 July 1916.

23. Ll Wyn Griffith, *Up to Mametz*, London 1931, p.194.

24. Evans MS.

25. WO95/2539, 38th Division War Diary. Appendices VII and X to

July volume: 38th Division Operation Order No. 36 and modifying order No.G260. The latter, which could give rise to misunderstanding (especially if looked at out of context) reads as follows:

For the first five lines (of Order No. 36) substitute:

> The general plan of attack will be: 115th Infantry Brigade will have two battalions in position in Caterpillar Wood by 2 am. A third battalion will be in Montauban Alley, and the fourth battalion near the Loop. The last two should be in position by 6 am.

In neither order is anything further said about the disposition of infantry battalions.

26. WO95/2560, 115th Infantry Brigade War Diary, appendix to July entries: Brigade Operation Order No. 62 (dated 6 July 1916).

27. WO95/5, GHQ War Diary. Appendix D to July 1916 entries: GHQ Meteorological Section Weather Diary.

28. Edmonds, *Official History* 1916 Vol. 2, p.30. The 17th Division War Diary (WO95/1981) gives a similar, though slightly less detailed, account.

29. Griffith, *Up to Mametz*, p.195.

30. Evans MS.

31. Griffith, *Up to Mametz*, pp.198-9. This account is confirmed by the 115th Brigade War Diary (WO95/2560) and other sources. Edmonds (op.cit.) attributes the lack of smoke to high winds but it seems more probable that it was due to lack of communication between brigade headquarters and the RE Stokes mortar unit despatched by corps headquarters to provide the smoke barrage. If high winds were the reason, brigade headquarters would have been made aware of it.

32. Marden, *History of the Welch Regiment 1914-1918*, pp.383-4.

33. William Joshua, letter to the author, January 1974.

34. WO95/2560, 115th Infantry Brigade War Diary.

35. C T Atkinson, *History of the South Wales Borderers*, London 1931, p.244. Atkinson says that the 10th SWB did not arrive until just before 3 pm but other sources - particularly the brigade diary - make it clear that they arrived sooner than this and were in action by 2.15 pm.

36. WO95/921, XV Corps War Diary: entries for 10.10 and 10.20am.

37. Griffith, *Up to Mametz*, p.199. The 115th Infantry Brigade diary records: 'at 10.25 am the GOC was informed that another artillery bombardment would take place at 10.45 and would last for half an hour'.
38. WO95/2560, 115th Infantry Brigade War Diary, Appendix XV: copy of wire from 38th Division timed 2.18 pm (but, according to the diary, not received until 4.04 pm).
39. Griffith, *Up to Mametz*, pp.200-1.
40 Evans MS, and 115th Infantry Brigade War Diary (WO95/2560)
41. WO95/921, XV Corps War Diary. Entry for 6.40 pm.
42. Griffith, *Up to Mametz*, pp.205-6.
43. CAB45/191, letter from Brig.-Gen. Trotter dated 2 April 1930.
44. WO95/1981, 17th Division War Diary. This account is reasonably consistent with that in the 50th Brigade diary (WO95/1998) and in the anonymous *History of the 50th Infantry Brigade 1914-1919*, printed for private circulation in 1919.
45. WO95/921, XV Corps War Diary. Entry for 4.05 pm.
46. Edmonds, *Official History* 1916 Vol. 2, p.31.
47. WO95/921, XV Corps War Diary. Entry for 10.52 pm.
48. WO95/2560, 115th Infantry Brigade War Diary, Annexes to July entries: OA 256 of 16 July 1916 from Lt.-Gen. Kiggell to all Armies; XV Corps No. 125G of 11 July 1916 to all divisions. Kiggell's note goes on to say:

> An infantry brigadier whose command has met with conspicuous success, ascribes it largely to the fact that his men have insisted in advancing close under the field artillery fire, even at the risk of an occasional casualty from our own guns. His men were thus enabled to gain an enemy's trench almost without loss and in time to meet the defenders hand to hand as they emerged from their dug-outs and before they could mount their machine guns.

This is an early example of the use of the 'creeping barrage' which was to be used so effectively later on.
49. WO95/921, XV Corps War Diary. Entry for 10.13 am.
50. Rawlins, Col. S W H, 'History of the Development of British Artillery in France'. Unpublished typescript in the Ministry of Defence library, p.104. This describes the main artillery lessons of the Battle of the Somme 'as deduced by

GOC RA Fourth Army'.

51. Evans MS. During his reconnaissance of Caterpillar Wood on 6 July, Evans had decided to place his headquarters somewhere in the trenches behind Caterpillar Wood and he was surprised when told later that day that he was to operate from Pommiers Redoubt over 1,000 yards away.

52. WO95/5, GHQ War Diary. General Staff entry for 9 July 1916.

53. Haig MS. Diary entry for 8 July 1916.

54. Rawlinson MS. Journal entry for 7 July 1916.

55. WO95/921, XV Corps, General Staff War Diary. Entry for 9.10pm on 7 July 1916.

56. ibid. Entry for 10.30 am on 8 July 1916.

57. ibid. Entry for 1.40 pm on 8 July 1916.

58. WO95/2552, 113th Infantry Brigade War Diary. Entry for 3 am on 9 July 1916.

59. Haig MS. Diary entry for 9 July. Haig's figure of 150 casualties is well below the true number. The Cardiff City battalion alone suffered 280 casualties, including six officers killed.

60. WO95/921, XV Corps War Diary. Entry for 10.20 am on 9 July 1916.

61. William George, *My Brother and I*, London 1958, p.255.

Notes on Chapter Four

Epigraph: David Jones, *In Parenthesis*, London 1937, p.165.

1. WO95/921, XV Corps War Diary, Appendix 61A/13: copy of 38th Division Order No. 38, issued at 2 am on 9 July 1916. This order gives two alternatives, pending the outcome of the 2 am attack on Strip Trench. The choice between them was made by Maj.-Gen. Philipps at 4 am.

2. WO95/921, XV Corps War Diary, Appendix 61A/13.

3. ibid. Appendix 61A/19: message to 17th and 38th Divisions from corps commander, issued 2 pm on 9 July 1916.

4. WO95/1981, 17th Division War Diary. Entry for 9/10 July. This was, in fact, the seventh attack on Quadrangle Support by the division which had paid dearly for this limited success.

5. T O Marden, *History of the Welch Regiment 1914-1918*, Cardiff 1932, p.384. Marden commanded the 114th Infantry

Brigade at Mametz Wood and his book therefore contains a first hand record of the battle.

6. WO95/921, XV Corps War Diary. Appendix 61A/23.

7. WO95/2539, 38th Division War Diary, Appendix X: 38th Division Order No. 30.

8. WO95/1639, Commander, Royal Artillery, 7th Division War Diary: Artillery Order No. 19a (modified), dated 9 July 1916. The technique of the 'feint' was not generally promulgated to British units until 11 July, when GHQ OA225 advocated its use and attributed its development to the French (copy in WO95/2560, 115th Infantry Brigade War Diary).

9. Compiled from the following sources:
   a. Mulmann und Mohs, *Geschichte des Lehr Infanterie Regiments*, Thuringen 1935, pp.278-302.
   b. Reichsarchivs monograph *Somme-Nord*: Band 20 in the series *Schlachten des Weltkrieges*, 1927 (map section following p.280).
   c. *Army Quarterly*, Vol. 9, No. 2, pp.245-59: 'The other side of the Hill' (from histories of the German 183rd, 184th, and 122nd Infantry regiments).

10. *Army Quarterly*, Vol. 9, No. 2, p.259, quoting the historian of the 183rd Infantry Regiment.

11. WO157/468, XV Corps Intelligence Summaries, 10 July 1916.

12. It might be helpful in understanding the battle to remember that all battalions of the 113th Brigade were Royal Welsh Fusiliers, and all battalions of the 114th Brigade were Welsh Regiment, viz:

113th Brigade	114th Brigade
13th RWF (1st North Wales)	10th Welsh (1st Rhondda)
14th RWF (Carnarvon & Anglesey)	13th Welsh (2nd Rhondda)
15th RWF (London Welsh)	14th Welsh (Swansea)
16th RWF (2nd North Wales)	15th Welsh (Carmarthen)

The 115th Brigade was a mixed brigade:
   10th SWB (1st Gwent)
   11th SWB (2nd Gwent)
   16th Welsh (Cardiff City)
   17th RWF

13. Jones, *In Parenthesis*, p.156.

14. Arthur Conan Doyle, *The British Campaign in France and Flanders 1916*, London 1918, p.126.

15. WO95/2556, 16th RWF War Diary, Appendix 1 to July entries: report by Major J R H McLellan.

16. C H D Ward, *Regimental Records of the Royal Welch Fusiliers 1914-1918*, London 1928, p.206.

17. ibid., p.206. Narrative account by Captain J Glynn Jones, 14th RWF.

18. T J Price, letter to the author, 26 January 1974.

19. Richard Lyons, notes written for the author in August 1972. Mr Lyons points out that only officers carried compasses which became scarce as officer casualties mounted.

20. Griffith Jones, letter to the author 1974.

21. Ward, *Regimental Records of the Royal Welch Fusiliers 1914-1918*, p.207.

22. Edmonds, *Official History* 1916 Vol. 2, p.51; also CRA 7th Division War Diary (WO95/1639), entry for 5.26 am on 10th July.

23. Haig MS. Diary entry for 10 July 1916.

24. The German account of the fighting in Mametz Wood on 10 July is from *Geschichte des Lehr Regiments*, pp.296-9.

25. WO95/2552, 113th Infantry Brigade War Diary, Appendix 15: Summary of the action at Mametz Wood by Brig.-Gen. Price-Davies (dated 14 July 1916).

26. David Jones, letter to the author dated 24 March 1971. Jones made use of this incident in his book, *In Parenthesis*:
    ...and Jesus Christ - they're coming through the floor
    endthwart and overlong:
    Jerry's through on the flank...and: Beat it! -
    That's what that one said as he ran past:
    Boches back in Strip Trench - it's a
    monumental bollocks every time...

27. WO95/2557, 114th Infantry Brigade War Diary, Appendix C: report on operations of 10/11 July by Brig.-Gen. Marden (dated 16 July).

28. WO95/921, XV Corps War Diary, Appendices B62/6 and 6A: messages to XV Corps from Fourth Army observation post and from XIII Corps headquarters.

29. *Army Quarterly*, Vol. 9, No. 2, 1925: 'The other side of the Hill' p.257.

30. Rawlinson MS. Journal entry for 10 July 1916.

31. Haig MS. Diary entry for 10 July 1916.

32. WO95/2560, 115th Infantry Brigade War Diary, entry for 11

July. Also Appendix IX: 115th Brigade Operation Order No. 64, dated 10 July, which begins: 'The Brigade will occupy and hold at all costs Mametz Wood'. Brigadier Evans was obviously unaware that the battalions in the wood had drawn back from the previous position 50 yards from the northern edge of the wood.

33. WO95/2557, 114th Infantry Brigade War Diary, Appendix C.

34. WO95/2560, 115th Infantry Brigade War Diary. Entry for 11 July.

35. Ll Wyn Griffith, *Up to Mametz*, London 1931, pp.208-13.

36. WO95/2560, 115th Infantry Brigade War Diary. Entry for 11 July 1916. Griffith uses identical wording, and must have had before him either the diary or the message itself when writing his account some years afterwards (*Up to Mametz*, p.218).

37. Griffith, *Up to Mametz*, p.219. The 16th Welsh and 11th SWB were 'fresh' only in the sense that they had not taken part in any fighting in the wood, but they were still recovering from their exertions of 7 July, and on 10 July they had been fetching and carrying for the 113th and 114th Brigades.

38. ibid., p.221. Unknown to Captain Griffith, one of the runners chosen to carry the message he had written was his younger brother, Private Watcyn Griffith of the 17th RWF. He was killed before he reached Queen's Nullah. Capt. Griffith heard the news a few hours later.

39. WO95/1639, Commander, Royal Artillery, 7th Division War Diary, entry for 11.15 am on 11 July 1916. See also War Diary of the 35th Brigade, Royal Field Artillery (WO95/1643). It is difficult to establish the exact time at which the barrage lifted but it is quite clear that it went on beyond 3 pm, the scheduled time for the infantry attack. The entry in the CRA, 7th Division diary says 'G [General Staff] order bombardment 2.45 - 3 pm on north edge of wood and 150 yards back. 21st Divn. artillery will bombard west of Railway, Pearl Wood and Alley. 80th, 35th and 122nd Brigades will bombard northern edge of wood, Flatiron and Sabot copses. All will lift at 3 pm on the German Second Line.' The official history says that interrupted telephone communications caused half an hour's delay: 'At 3.30 pm the British artillery ceased firing on the northern edge of the

wood'. The 115th Infantry Brigade diary also says that the bombardment lasted until 3.30 pm, but the diary of the 35th Brigade RFA, 7th Division, records that their batteries 'bombarded northern edge of Mametz Wood...till 3.15 pm'.

40. WO95/1643, 22nd Brigade, Royal Field Artillery, War Diary. Entry for 11 July 1916: 'Fighting in Mametz Wood still continues but our advance has now progressed so far that batteries are becoming out of range'.

41. WO95/2560, 115th Infantry Brigade War Diary. Entry for 11 July 1916.

42. ibid.

43. Mulmann und Mohs, *Geschichte des Lehr Infanterie Regiments*, p.293.

44. WO95/2560, 115th Infantry Brigade War Diary. The diary records that at 4 pm, German prisoners from the 77th Regiment and 122nd Regiment were taken who stated that '1000 men had been thrown into the wood on the night of 10/11 July'.

45. Mulmann und Mohs, *Geschichte des Lehr Infanterie Regiments*, p.300.

46. WO95/921, XV Corps War Diary. Appendix 63/7.

47. WO95/2539, 38th Division War Diary. Appendix 12.

48. Griffith, *Up to Mametz*, p231-4.

49. Edmonds, *Official History* 1916 Vol. 2, p.54.

50. Figures are from Marden, *History of the Welch Regiment 1914-1918*, p.390. Marden also gives figures for each battalion of the Welsh Regiment involved in the fighting (but not for battalions of the other two regiments represented in the division). These figures are approximately the same as those recorded in the battalion diaries. It has not been possible to check Marden's figure for the division as a whole as the complete casualty figures for all the RWF battalions are not recorded. There is no reason to doubt the figure of about 4,000 which is also given in the official history.

51. William Joshua, letter to the author dated 25 January 1974.

Notes on Chapter Five

Epigraph: David Jones, *In Parenthesis*, London 1937, p.164.

1. WO95/431, Fourth Army papers, File A (Fourth Army Operation Orders
   1-31 July 1916): 'Brief Account of the Operations of the Fourth Army on 14 July 1916'.
2. CAB45/190, letter from Gen. Sir A A Montgomery-Massingham dated 22 April 1931.
3. B H Liddell Hart, *History of the First World War*, London 1930, p.246.
4. WO95/431: as note 1.
5. ibid.
6. Brig.-Gen. Sir James Edmonds, *Official History* 1916 Vol.2, p.78.
7. WO95/431 and Edmonds, *Official History* 1916 Vol. 2, p.85.
8. WO95/431, Fourth Army papers.
9. Edmonds, *Official History* 1916 Vol. 2, p.89 (based on German sources).
10. Liddell Hart, *History of the First World War*, p.248.
11. George A B Dewar and Lt.Col. J H Boraston, *Sir Douglas Haig's Command*, London 1922, Vol. 1, pp.113-6. Boraston wrote the chapter from which the quotation is taken.
12. ibid., p.113.
13. Rawlinson MS. Item 87d: Kiggell to Rawlinson, 8 July 1916.
14. ibid. Journal entry for 7 July 1916.
15. CAB45/189, letter from Major G P L Drake-Brockman dated 7 February 1930.
16. Edmonds, *Official History* 1916 Vol. 2, p.16.
17. ibid., p.17.
18. ibid., p.65.
19. ibid. By inspection from Index to Arms, formations and units, pp.593-4.
20. CAB45/190, letter from Brig.-Gen. L A E Price-Davies, 6 March 1930.
21. WO95/2552, 113th Infantry Brigade War Diary, Appendix 20, July 1916: message dated 16 July 1916.
22. ibid. Appendix 18, dated 23 July 1916.
23. ibid. Appendix 26, dated 20 July 1916: Report by Brig.-Gen. Price-Davies to 38th Division headquarters. No trace can be found of the previous report of 15 July to which Price-Davies refers.
24. CAB45/189, letter from Captain J Glynn Jones dated 28 April

1930, with notes.

25. CAB45/189, letter from Major Drake-Brockman dated 7 February 1930, with notes. The notes contain several errors, particularly where reference is made to corps and battalion numbers, which is not perhaps surprising as they were written nearly 14 years after the events described. From the descriptive matter it is however easy to detect the errors and make allowances accordingly. For example, Lt.Col. David Davies was OC 14th RWF, not 16th RWF as stated by Drake-Brockman. As Drake-Brockman joined the division after Davies had left for England, his assessment of Davies's capabilities must be based on hearsay.

26. *The Times*, 11 July 1916.

27. CAB45/189, letter from Lt.Col. G H Gwyther OC 14th RWF, dated 21 April 1930. Gwyther, however, attributes the mistakes to brigade orders.

28. CAB45/189, letter from Captain J Glynn Jones.

29. Siegfried Sassoon, *Memoirs of an Infantry Officer*, London 1930, p.71.

30. Gerald Brenan, *A Life of One's Own*, London 1962, pp.205-6.

31. Frank Delamain [ed.], *Going Across: Extracts from the war letters and diary of Lt. St. H Evans*, Newport (undated), p.46.

32. D V Kelly, *39 Months*, London 1930 (though written in 1919), pp.28-9.

33. Frank Richards, *Old Soldiers Never Die*, London 1933, p.181.

34. Robert Graves, *Goodbye to All That*, London 1929, p.175 (Penguin edition). The stinking German corpse is also the subject of Graves's poem 'Dead Boche'.

35. WO95/2557, 114th Infantry Brigade War Diary.

36. ibid. Appendix C, 16 July 1916.

37. CAB45/190, letter from Brig.-Gen. Marden, dated 27 March 1930.

38. CAB45/190, letter from Maj.-Gen. Pilcher written in 1930.

39. WO95/2560, 115th Infantry Brigade War Diary. Entry for 7-12 July 1916. (My emphasis.)

40. CAB45/189, letter from Lt.Col. Gwyther.

41. Jones, *In Parenthesis*, p.148.

42. Ll Wyn Griffith, *Up to Mametz*, London 1931, p.207.

43. Sgt. T H Davies, 13th RWF. Letter to the author dated 24 January 1974. And cf. the cockney character in David Jones's *In Parenthesis*, p.138:

> There was some bastard wood as Jerry was sitting tight in and this mob clickt for the job of asking him to move on - if you please - an' thank you very much indeed, signally obliged to yer, Jerry-boy.

44. CAB45/189, letter from Lt.Col. Gwyther.
45. ibid., letter from Captain Glynn Jones.
46. Kelly, *39 Months*, p.159.
47. A J P Taylor, *The First World War*, London 1963, p.140 (Penguin edition).
48. ibid.
49. Mulmann und Mohs, *Geschichte des Lehr Infanterie Regiments*, Thuringen, 1935, pp.319-20.
50. Edmonds, *Official History* 1916 Vol. 2, p.204.
51. *The Times*, 21 August 1916.

ANNEX A

II3th INF. BDE. OPERATION ORDER 100

MANOEUVRES

Ref: Sheet 36b 1/40,000

1. The brigade will capture the enemy's 2nd line system between the points U.3b-O.34c and the 3rd line system between the points U.4c and U.4b. These objectives are to be regarded as strictly limited except that commanders should extend to their flanks to secure their position should the attack of troops on their flank or flanks fail, or lose direction.
2. The second line system will be attacked by the 13th battalion RWF on the right, and the 16th battalion RWF on the left.
3. This attack will leave the German 1st line system at 2 pm in eight lines at 30 paces distance in accordance with the organisation already issued. Four machine guns will accompany the sixth line.
4. When information has been received that the above objective has been reached, the 14th and 15th battalions RWF on the right and left respectively will leave the German front line system in artillery formation.
5. Before leaving the valley in rear of the 2nd line system, lines will be formed (as already stated), and the advance will move over the 2nd line system to the attack of the 3rd line system. Four machine guns will accompany this attack.
6. The artillery will lift 15 minutes after this attack leaves the valley in the rear of the 2nd line system. Every means of sending this information back must be employed, as smoke, etc. may prevent the advance being actually seen.
7. Eight machine guns will be used to provide overhead fire to support the attacks and will form a reserve in the hands of the brigadier.
8. All positions gained will be consolidated. One section of RE will be sent forward to each battalion after it has gained its objective.

9. It is important that touch should be maintained both laterally and from front to rear. All ranks will watch for runners and assist them, and forward their messages if they become casualties. Runners will wear white armbands. Two runners from each battalion will report for duty at brigade headquarters at 1 pm.

10. Watches will be synchronised at 10.15 am at brigade headquarters. (In theory only; it will actually be done at the conference at 10.15 am.)

11. Reports will be sent to crossroads at U.31.b.6.4., where brigade headquarters will be situated at first. Brigade headquarters will be advanced as the situation allows.

12. Attention is directed to instructions already issued (BM6194).

13. The 129th Field Ambulance will establish a dressing station in Monchy le Breton.

14. Battalions taking prisoners will arrange to escort them back to brigade headquarters. Escorts should be in a strength of one to ten prisoners.

15. 113th Trench Mortar Battery will send one Stokes gun forward in rear of each battalion. Remainder of battery to remain in reserve in 1st line German trenches.

22 June 1916.   (Sgd.) H Hodson, Major
                                        for Brigade Major
                                        113th Infantry Brigade.

[Source: WO95/2551 (Brigade War Diary)]

ANNEX B

38th (WELSH) DIVISION ORDER NO.39

9 July 1916

1. The division will attack Mametz Wood tomorrow with a view to capturing the whole of it. Throughout the operation the left of the 114th Infantry Brigade, and the right of the 113th Infantry Brigade will be on the main ride running north and south through Mametz Wood. The 17th Division will cooperate by bombing up Quadrangle Support and Wood Support. The hour of the infantry assault on the edge of the wood will be 4.15 am, but all troops will be ready in position by 3 am.

2. From 3.30 am to 4.15 am the artillery will bombard the southern portion of Mametz Wood, especially the edge of the wood J.H.G.E.B.A.X.

3. At 3.55 am a smoke barrage will be formed in the neighbourhood of Strip Trench and at A.B.C.X., and will be continued for 30 minutes.

4. At 4.15 am the artillery will lift gradually to a barrage north and west of the J.F. line - D - X, maintaining a barrage on Wood Support, and (under cover of the smoke barrage) the 114th Infantry Brigade will attack the front X.A.G., and the 113th Infantry Brigade will attack between G and Strip Trench, pushing on to the first objective - a line just short of the ride running east from Wood Support - and B.C.X. Strong points will be immediately made near A.B.C.X., eastern edge of ride near the main central ride at X.24.c.,5.8 and at junction of Wood Trench with Strip Trench, and eastern edge of Wood Support.

5. At 6.15 am the artillery barrage will lift to the line W.V.Y.O. and K., and the infantry will capture and consolidate the line, making strong points at V.Y.O. and K.

6. At 7.15 am the artillery barrage will be lifted to north edge of the wood U to P, and the infantry will advance and consolidate themselves inside the north edge of the wood, making strong points near U.T.S.R.A. and P.

7. At 8.15 am the artillery barrage will be lifted on to the German second line.

8. Throughout the operation machine gun fire will be directed
    from Marlboro' Wood and Caterpillar Wood in a north westerly
    direction against Middle Alley to prevent communication
    between the German second line and Mametz Wood. This area
    will also be kept under constant artillery fire.

9. Three heavy trench mortars in Queens Nullah and the medium
    trench mortars in Cliff Trench will assist the attack against
    Strip Trench. Care should be taken as regards Wood Trench
    which is occupied by the 17th Division up to within 50 yards
    of its junction with Strip Trench. GOC 113th Infantry Brigade
    will arrange for close and constant communication with the
    right battalion of the 17th Division. A heavy mortar will be
    placed in position today to bombard the portion of the wood
    A.B.C.X. GOC 114th Infantry Brigade will also place light
    mortars to assist in bombarding this portion of the wood.

10. The 124th Fd. Coy. R.E. and two companies pioneers have been
    placed at the disposal of the GOC 113th Infantry Brigade to
    make strong points and dig a trench from Strip Trench to
    Cliff Trench. 151st Fd. Coy. R.E. and pioneers less two
    companies are placed at the disposal of GOC 114th Infantry
    Brigade to make strong points, and a communication trench
    from neighbourhood of Caterpillar Wood to Mametz Wood. 123rd.
    Fd. Coy. R.E. will be in reserve at present billets (F.28.b.,
    1.6).

11. The 115th Infantry Brigade less two companies at Caterpillar
    Wood will be in reserve near Minden Post.

12. C.R.E. will arrange for necessary R.E. material being brought
    up rapidly as required from depots at Queens Nullah and
    Caterpillar Wood, 115th Infantry Brigade furnishing carrying
    parties as required. Divisional headquarters will be informed
    by C.R.E. of the numbers used as carriers.

13. GOC 113th Infantry Brigade will form an ammunition, ration
    and water depot near Queens Nullah, and GOC 114th Infantry
    Brigade similar depots by White Trench and Caterpillar Wood.

14. All men must be carefully instructed in the compass direction
    of the advance, and of the necessity for consolidation and
    reorganisation when the various rides and edges of the wood
    are reached. Care must be taken also to instruct in the
    advantage of working up as close as possible to the edge of
    our artillery barrage, and it should be explained to the men
    that artillery fire will sound much louder in the wood than

outside. To help the men in knowing which is the main central ride, GOC 113th Infantry Brigade will arrange for a party to place red flags along it. 25 flags will be issued to representatives of the brigade at the Halte at 9 pm today.

15. Brigade and battalion commanders will ensure that adequate arrangements have been made for intercommunication by visual and runners, as well as by wire. Immediate reports will be sent when each objective has been gained, otherwise hourly reports must be furnished of the progress being. Negative reports required.

> (Signed) H E Pryce
> Lieut. Col.
> General Staff 38th (Welsh) Division

ACKNOWLEDGE
Issued at: 5.30 pm

[Source: WO95/2539 (38th Division War Diary)]

Bibliography

1. Private Papers.

Evans MS: Personal notes by Brig.-Gen. H J Evans on operations about Mametz Wood. Generously presented to the author by Mr Peter Evans. Now in the Royal Welch Fusiliers Museum at Caernarfon.

Haig MS: Papers of Earl Haig of Bermersyde at the National Library of Scotland.

Lloyd George MS: Papers of David Lloyd George formerly at the Beaverbrook Library, now at the House of Lords.

Rawlinson MS: War journal of Lord Rawlinson of Trent and associated papers at Churchill College, Cambridge.

Letters from Private Will Jones (16th RWF) to his parents, 1915-1916 (in Welsh). In the possession of Miss Winifred Jones.

Letters to the author from survivors of the fighting at Mametz Wood:

W H Bampfield (16th Welsh); A H Bury (16th RWF); G H Crick (14th Welsh); J E Davies (13th RWF); T H Davies (13th RWF); E M Edwards (14th RWF); Ll. Wyn Griffith (15th RWF); H Iball (13th RWF); David Jones (15th RWF); E Jones (16th Welsh); G J Jones (16th RWF); W B Joshua (16th Welsh); G C Longworth; R Lyons (14th Welsh); R N Morgan (16th Welsh); L E Morley (11th SWB); A Parry (16th RWF); T J Price (13th Welsh); A F Richards (16th Welsh); T J Richards (16th Welsh); M R Roberts (14th RWF); R G Robinson (13th Welsh); C B Thomas (RFA); P S Williams (14th RWF).

2. Public Record Office papers

CAB45/188-191. Committee of Imperial Defence, Historical Section: additions and corrections to draft chapters of the official history proposed by surviving officers, including many from the 38th (Welsh) Division, in 1930. Some of the letters are accompanied by detailed notes.

WO95. War Diaries, especially the following:

WO95/

5. GHQ. General Staff.
431. Fourth Army. General Staff.
881. XI Corps. General Staff.
921. XV Corps. General Staff.
1631. 7th Division. General Staff.
1639. 7th Division. Commander, Royal Artillery.
1643. 7th Division. 22nd and 35th Brigades RFA.
1981. 17th Division. General Staff.
1998. 17th Division. 50th Inf. Bde. Headquarters.
2005. 17th Division. 51st Inf. Bde. Headquarters.
2009. 17th Division. 52nd Inf. Bde. Headquarters.
2130. 21st Division. General Staff.
2151. 21st Division. 62nd Inf. Bde. Headquarters.
2159. 21st Division. 64th Inf. Bde. Headquarters.
2163. 21st Division. 100th Inf. Bde. Headquarters.
2539. 38th Division. General Staff.
2542. 38th Division. Commander, Royal Artillery.
2551. 38th Division. 113th Inf. Bde. Headquarters.
2552. 38th Division. 113th Inf. Bde. Headquarters [cont.]
2555. 38th Division. 113th Inf. Bde. 13th & 14th RWF.
2556. 38th Division. 113th Inf. Bde. 15th & 16th RWF.
2557. 38th Division. 114th Inf. Bde. Headquarters.
2559. 38th Division. 114th Inf. Bde. 10th 13th 14th 15th Welsh.
2560. 38th Division. 115th Inf. Bde. Headquarters.
2561. 38th Division. 115th Inf. Bde. 17th RWF 16th Welsh.
2562. 38th Division. 115th Inf. Bde. 10th 11th SWB.
WO157/468.XV Corps Intelligence Summaries.

3. Official documents, handbooks etc.

Army Orders 1914.
Army Lists 1914-1916.
Field Service Pocket Book, HMSO, 1914.
Handbook of the German Army in War, HMSO, 1918.
Parliamentary Debates, *Official Report*, House of Commons 4th and 5th series.

Parliamentary Papers: Cmnd 2993. *Memorandum on Army Reorganisation*, 30 July 1906.

Statistics of the Military Effort of the British Empire during the Great War, HMSO, 1922.

4. Newspapers.

Carnarvon and Denbigh Herald	*South Wales Daily News*
Daily News and Leader	*The Times*
Liverpool Daily Post and Mercury	*Western Mail*

5. Autobiographies, Memoirs, Published Letters, Diaries etc.

Blake, Robert, *The Private Papers of Douglas Haig 1914-1919*, London 1952.

Blunden, Edmond, *Undertones of War*, London 1928.

Brenan, Gerald, *A Life of One's Own*, London 1962.

Chapman, Guy, *A Passionate Prodigality*, London 1933.

Delamain, Frank [ed.], *Going Across: Extracts from the war letters and diaries of Lt. St. H Evans*, Newport (undated).

George, William, *My Brother and I*, London 1958.

Gladden, Norman, *The Somme 1916*, London 1974.

Graves, Robert, *Goodbye to All That*, London 1929.

Grey of Falloden, *Twenty-Five Years*, London 1925.

Griffith, Ll Wyn, *Up to Mametz*, London 1931.

Haldane, R B, *Autobiography*, London 1929.

Hankey, Lord, *The Supreme Command*, Vol. 2, London 1961.

Jones, David, *In Parenthesis*, London 1937.

Kelly, D V, *39 Months*, London 1930.

Lloyd George, David, *War Memoirs*, London 1933-36.

Lloyd George Frances, *The Years that are Past*, London 1967.

Masefield, John, *The Old Front Line*, London 1917.

Montague, C E, *Disenchantment*, London 1922.

Morgan, Kenneth O [ed.], *Lloyd George: Family Letters 1885-1936*, Cardiff and London 1973.

Richards, Frank, *Old Soldiers Never Die*, London 1933.

Robertson, Sir William, *Private to Field Marshal*, London 1921.

Sassoon, Siegfried, *Memoirs of an Infantry Officer*, London 1930.

Sassoon, Siegfried, *Siegfried's Journey*, London 1945.

Taylor, A J P [ed.], *Lloyd George: A diary by Frances Stevenson*, London 1971.

Wilson, Trevor [ed.], *The Political Diaries of CP Scott, 1911-1928*, London 1970.

6. Biographies.

Bonham-Carter, Victor, *Soldier True: The Life and Times of Field-Marshal Sir William Robertson*, London 1963.

Cooper, A Duff, *Haig*, 2 Vols., London 1935-6.

Esher, Viscount, *The Tragedy of Lord Kitchener*, London 1921.

Fraser, Peter, *Lord Esher: A Political Biography*, London 1973.

Magnus, Philip, *Kitchener: Portrait of an Imperialist*, London 1958.

Marshal-Cornwall, James, *Haig as a Military Commander*, London 1974.

Maurice, Sir Frederick, *The Life of Viscount Haldane of Cloan*, London 1937.

Robbins, Keith, *Sir Edward Grey*, London 1971.

Roskill, Stephen, *Hankey*, Vol. 1, 1877-1918, London 1970.

Rowland, Peter, *Lloyd George*, London 1971.

Terraine, John, *Douglas Haig. The educated soldier*, London 1963.

7. Official, Divisional, Brigade and Regimental Histories.

Anon., *History of the 50th Infantry Brigade*. Printed for limited circulation 1919.

Anon., *Schlachten des Weltkrieges. Band 20: Somme-Norde*, Reichsarchiv 1927.

Anon., *Welsh Army Corps Executive Committee Report 1914-1919*, Cardiff 1921.

Atkinson, C T, *History of the South Wales Borderers 1914-1918*, London 1931.

Atteridge, A H, *History of the 17th (Northern) Division*, Glasgow 1929.

Baker, Harold, *The Territorial Force: A manual of its Law, Organisation and Administration*, London 1909.

Becke, A F, *History of the Great War Based on Official Documents: Order of Battle of Divisions*, London 1938.

Dunlop, Col. J K, *Development of the British Army 1899-1914*, London 1938.

Edmonds, Brig.-Gen. Sir J E, *History of the Great War Based on Official Documents: Military Operations. France and Belgium*, especially 1914 Vol. 1 and 1916 Vols. 1, 2 and Appendices, 1922-1938.

Germains, V W, *The Kitchener Armies*, London 1930.

Marden, T O, *History of the Welch Regiment 1914-1918*, Cardiff 1932.

Mulmann und Mohs, *Geschichte des Lehr Infanterie Regiments*, Thuringen 1935.

Munby, J E, *A History of the 38th (Welsh) Division*, London 1920.

Rawlins, Col. S W H, 'History of the Development of British Artillery in France'. Unpublished typescript in the Ministry of Defence library (undated).

Ward, C H D, *Regimental Records of the Royal Welch Fusiliers 1914-1918*, London 1928.

Williams, Capt. B, *Raising and Training the New Armies*, London 1918.

Wyrall, Everard, *The History of the 19th Division 1914-1918*, London (undated, but before 1932).

8. Articles.

Anon., 'Other Side of the Hill' (based on German Regimental Histories): *Army Quarterly*, Vol. 7, No. 2, 1924, and Vol. 9, No. 2, 1925.

Bond, Brian, 'The Territorial Army in Peace and War', *History Today*, Vol. XVI, No. 3, 1966.

9. General.

Chapman, Guy [ed.], *Vain Glory*, London 1968.

Churchill, Winston, *The World Crisis*, London 1923-31.

Cruttwell, C R M F, *A History of the Great War*, Oxford 1936.

Dewar, George A B, and Boraston, Lt.Col. J H, *Sir Douglas Haig's Command*, London 1922.

Doyle, Arthur Conan, *The British Campaign in France and Flanders*, London 1918.

Falls, Cyril, *The First World War*, London 1960.

Farrar-Hockley, A H, *The Somme*, London 1954.

Guinn, Paul, *British Strategy and Politics 1914 to 1918*, Oxford 1965.

Hazelhurst, Cameron, *Politicians at War, July 1914 to May 1915*, London 1971.

Liddell-Hart, B H, *History of the First World War*, London 1930 (as *The Real War*).

Middlebrook, Martin, *The First Day on the Somme*, London 1971.

Morgan, Kenneth O, *Wales in British Politics 1886-1922*, Cardiff 1970.

Nicholson, I, and Lloyd-Williams, T, *Wales: Its part in the War*, London 1919.

Panichas, George A [ed.], *Promise of Greatness*, London 1968.

Taylor, A J P, *The First World War*, London 1963.